Zodiac Self-Care Guide: Aries

(A Lifestyle Blueprint for Aries)

Unlock Nature's Secrets from the Sun, Moon, Zodiac Elements, Crystals, Gemstones, Herbs, Essential Oils, Chakras, and Daily Mantras and Affirmations, Perfectly Aligned for ARIES

Oonah Mae Platt

Published by **JKK Books & Media,** USA
First printing edition, 2024 in the United States

Dedication

To my inner child and our lifetime journey together to find the best version of me.

Contents

Aries

The Zodiac Elements Classification

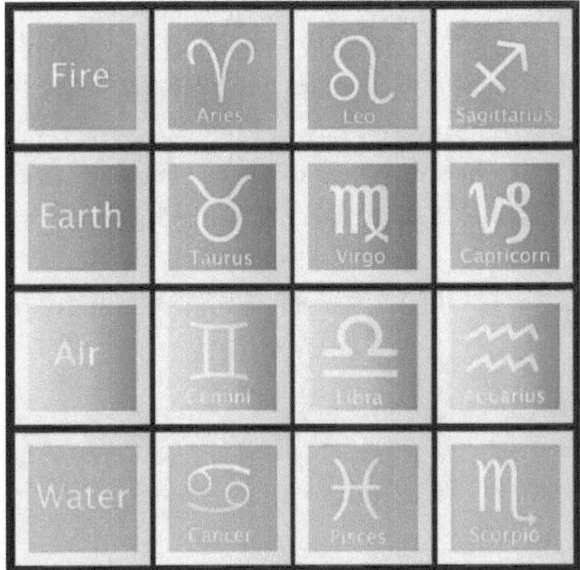

Acknowledgments

I want to express my utmost gratitude to my family, especially my children, for the sacrifices they made throughout the struggles of writing this book. They were supportive through the late nights and the writer's block I faced, like most authors, as I pressed on to the finish line. I also appreciate the guidance provided by my astrologer as I explored the intricacies involved in interpreting birth charts and understanding the interconnectivity of energies and elements in the bigger picture of our universe. Lastly, I thank my sister Vivienne "Mimi" for her prayers and for the ideas she presented regarding design concepts for the book covers.

Without all of you, this journey would have been twice as hard.

Introduction

If you purchased or were gifted this book, you are most likely an Aries, desiring to learn more about who you are, why you are the way you are, and how to use such knowledge about your personality to create the best possible life for yourself. Perhaps you are at a pivotal stage in your life and are interested in discovering how to choose a fulfilling career or ideal life partner. Or maybe you simply have an unsettling feeling, a restlessness, like something is missing from your life, and you are searching for your spiritual destiny. Regardless of the reason or motivation that brought you to this point, rest assured that you have made the right decision: **You have chosen the right book** to address all your questions and curiosities.

This book is all about Aries, the first sign of the zodiac. For anyone whose birthday falls between March 21 and April 19, you're in for a treat! You are an Aries, and this book is all about you: understanding yourself, learning how to take the best care of yourself, and bringing out the best of your personality.

This book is divided into two parts. Part One comprises chapters one through four and focuses on studying and understanding yourself as an Aries. In the first chapter, you will learn all about the birth period that designates you as an Aries, as well as the Aries symbols and meanings. The second chapter dives into the element that rules Aries and how it shapes your nature and behavior. Chapter Three is all about the celestial influences active in Aries: the ruling planet, the sun's impact on your ego, and the moon's role in regulating your emotions. As we move on to Chapter Four, the last chapter in Part One, you will discover your characteristic strengths and appreciate your weaknesses as an Aries. You will also learn how to overcome common challenges faced by Aries personalities.

Part Two includes chapters five through ten. Chapter Five is a fun chapter that walks you through the essential and unique tools used for Aries self-care, including chakra energies, power colors, crystals and gemstones, herbs and essential oils, and any symbolic talismans or familial animals. Chapter Six focuses solely on chakra self-care recommendations for the Aries individual. Chapter Seven explores the best career choices for Aries, while Chapter Eight tackles love and relationships and provides tips for finding the ideal romantic partners. Chapter Nine covers recommended self-care practices for Aries, including mantras, daily affirmations, and biblical support for the Aries personality. It also offers suggestions for harnessing your chakra-healing energy. The final chapter of the book, Chapter Ten, summarizes everything you have learned into a succinct, one-page table for easy reference. A conclusion follows and reflects on your journey throughout the book.

It is essential to understand that this book goes beyond the constellation of Aries, the associated elements, and so on. It is designed to help you harness the full potential of your Aries spirit in every area of your life, from career to relationships and from self-care to personal growth. The goal is for this book to serve as a road map for you to live more authentically as an Aries by helping you understand and take care of yourself better, connect with others more intensely, or simply embrace your unique essence as an Aries. So, buckle up, and let's embark on this journey together, unlocking the secrets of the zodiac's most courageous sign, one page at a time!

Part One

Self-Study

"We are born at a given moment in a given place and, like vintage wine, we possess the qualities of the year and of the season in which we are born."

— Carl Jung

Chapter 1

What defines an Aries?

1.1 Astrology as the basis of the Zodiac system.

Hello, dear Aries! Have you ever wondered why you do certain things the way you do or why you seem to be attracted to the same personality types? Have you pondered why most of the clothes and accessories in your closet are all in shades of the same color, say red, for example, even though you cannot consciously recall choosing the same colors whenever you shop? Perhaps you may have asked yourself multiple times why you cannot seem to find the "right job" even though you appear to excel at your current one to all intents and purposes. Furthermore, like me, you may have found yourself inexplicably propelled toward a specific career that seemed to call out to you. The above scenarios are some of the reasons why humans have sought, for millions of years, to understand and unravel the complexities of the human personality and the influences of the cosmic universe on us. In simple terms, the study of the positions and movements of celestial bodies such as the sun, moon, stars, and planets, as well as their influences on the earth, human life, and personality traits, is termed astrology. Astrology, in turn, forms the basis for mapping the zodiac signs.

Let's begin with a brief introduction to the origin of astrology as the basis for the development of the Zodiac signs. Astrology originated in ancient Babylon around the second millennium BCE and was initially used to predict seasonal shifts. Since then, it has expanded and evolved through many decades into a complex system that utilizes the twelve zodiac signs to categorize and predict human behavior. Although it is classified as a pseudoscience by the scientific community, astrology remains popular in the New Age and contemporary culture. According to the American best-selling author and astrologer Stephen Arroyo (2012), astrology is described as a language of energy, with the zodiac signs as energy patterns and the planets as energy regulators. Based on this definition, we can formulate a mental picture of the interaction of the pillars of astrology. Building upon this energy belief system, every person has a unique energy blueprint imprinted on them at birth. This energy signature captures the distinct pattern of alignment of the celestial constellation (sun, moon, stars, and planets) at the specific moment of their birth. This unique energy pattern influences the person's entire life by shaping their personality traits, which, in turn, affects how the person interacts with and responds to the rest of the world. Therefore, it makes sense that by understanding these characteristics and influences that are unique to your zodiac personality, you can understand your strengths and weaknesses and utilize the knowledge in daily self-care to create a fulfilling life for yourself.

1.2 Astrology versus Astronomy

Before going further, I think it is necessary to clarify some key terms that will appear frequently in this exciting adventure. In everyday language, astrology is often used interchangeably with astronomy, but in reality, both terms are different. The most notable difference between the two terms is that astronomy is considered a science, whereas astrology is regarded as a belief system.

Astrology: Astrology is defined as the belief that the positioning of the stars, planets, moon, sun, and other celestial bodies affects the occurrence of events on Earth (American Astronomical Society, n.d.). The study of astrology relies on the assumption or belief that specific time periods in the universe are associated with characteristic and distinguishable qualities/attributes that manifest in the personality and fate of individuals born during those periods (Perry, n.d.). Astrologers believe that the relative positions and movements of celestial objects, such as the sun, moon, stars, and planets, can influence people and events on Earth. Based on this belief, astrologers use the positions of these celestial objects to explain or predict human behavior and events occurring on Earth. Generally, astrology is classified as a pseudoscience because there is no scientific evidence to support this belief system (that is, astrology lacks a scientific basis). This belief system has been described as a "divinatory belief system."

Astronomy: On the other hand, the American Astronomical Society (n.d.) defines astronomy as the scientific study of the universe (including the planets, stars, galaxies, and other celestial constellations), which involves using mathematics, physics, and chemistry to determine the origins, behaviors, and relationships of these objects with each other. Unlike astrology, astronomy is classified as a scientific discipline.

Constellation(s): The Lunar and Planetary Institute (LPI) describes a constellation as a group of stars that appear to form a pattern or picture when seen against the dark background of the night sky. There are 88 "official" constellations recognized by the American Astronomical Society (AAS).

Zodiac: The word "zodiac" comes from the Greek word ζῳδιακός (zōidiakos), which translates literally as "circle of animals." Subsequently, the Latin term for zodiac, *zōdiacus,* was derived from the original Greek word (*Zodiac Constellations | Constellation Guide,* n.d.). Based on the origin of the word, it is therefore not surprising that seven of the zodiac constellations are represented by animals just as they did during the Greek and Roman era when they were conceived: Aries (the Ram), Taurus (the Bull), Cancer (the Crab), Leo (the Lion), Scorpius (the Scorpion), Capricornus (the Goat), and Pisces (the Fish).

Zodiac system: The Zodiac system is defined by Sutter (2024) as an imaginary, loose collection of constellations that the Sun passes through every year and which is used by astrologers to predict the lives and future of humans on Earth. Another source, the Merriam-Webster dictionary, describes the Zodiac system as an imaginary band in the heavens that contains the presumed travel paths of the sun and all the planets and is divided into twelve (12) star constellations or signs (12 Zodiac signs) for astrological purposes. The 12-star constellations within the zodiac family are: Aries, Taurus, Gemini, Cancer, Leo, Virgo, Libra, Scorpio, Sagittarius, Capricorn, Aquarius, and Pisces. Based on directions and location, the twelve zodiac constellations can further be divided into two: - the **northern** zodiac constellations (comprising Aries, Taurus, Gemini, Cancer, Leo, and Pisces), which are located in the **eastern** celestial hemisphere; AND - the **southern** zodiac constellations (Libra, Scorpio, Sagittarius, Capricorn, Aquarius, and Virgo), which are located in the **western** celestial hemisphere.

1.3 The debate over date variations within the Zodiac System

In 2011, a news report aired on CBS News in Baltimore shocked the entire nation. According to the news reporter for the story, Mary Bubala, astronomers had concluded from extensive data analysis that a shift in the Earth's alignment has changed zodiac dates and even added a new sign. This news story triggered a debate that has consumed horoscope watchers worldwide. Today, it is not unusual to find astrology charts, books, or publications that list dates or time frames for the Zodiac system that differ by a day or two in either direction. The date variation is not an error, nor does it undermine the publication's authenticity. Instead, the date variation has been explained to be the result of the Earth's axial rotation (remember from your high school geography or science class that the Earth rotates/spins on its axis, which produces the various seasonal changes we witness here on Earth). This axial rotation of the Earth causes our view of the constellations (stars, moon, and sun) to slowly shift over time, resulting in slightly changing dates for the Zodiac system over time. Astronomers and scientists describe this phenomenon as precession. It is considered a prolonged process that takes thousands of years to produce a noticeable physical change in the positions of these constellations and a resultant change in the positions of the Zodiac system. Precession implies that the Earth's position relative to the sun, the moon, and the stars has changed significantly and is no longer the same as during the Babylonian Era when the Zodiac system was first established. Over long time periods (thousands of years), these positional "shifts" have caused the dates of the Zodiac system to be "off" from what we once knew. Due to the effects of precession, some astronomers have proposed that the dates for the Zodiac signs within the Zodiac system should be corrected to account for the shifts among the constellations and that when this is done, it will potentially add a thirteenth (13th) Zodiac sign which has been designated as "Ophiuchus." Sounds weird, right? You are not alone in thinking this way. Most of the public's response to this phenomenon has mainly been unacceptance or outright rejection. Jim O'Leary of the Maryland Science Center explained that how astrologers interpret and depict horoscopes is not scientifically correct because it does not match exactly where the sun's location and influences exist in relation to the other constellations in the sky. In response, the astrology community points out that the current effects of precession in the present world do not influence or change the Zodiac signature that was present at the time of a person's birth, say 10, 20, or 30 years ago. This is also a valid point, in my opinion. However, you be the judge for yourself.

Most horoscope publishers today continue to publish horoscopes under the original Babylonian-based alignment, and they have no plans to change to the new astronomy-proposed alignment in the near future.

SIGNS OF THE ZODIAC

NUMBER	NAME	SYMBOL	SUN ENTERS[1]
1	Aries the Ram	♈	March 21
2	Taurus the Bull	♉	April 20
3	Gemini the Twins	♊	May 21
4	Cancer the Crab	♋	June 22
5	Leo the Lion	♌	July 23
6	Virgo the Virgin	♍	August 23
7	Libra the Balance	♎	September 23
8	Scorpio the Scorpion	♏	October 24
9	Sagittarius the Archer	♐	November 22
10	Capricorn the Goat	♑	December 22
11	Aquarius the Water Bearer	♒	January 20
12	Pisces the Fishes	♓	February 19

[1] Though no longer astronomically accurate (because of precession of the equinoxes), these traditional dates continue to be used in astrology.

The Babylonians divided the zodiac into 12 equal parts, each covering 30° of celestial longitude, around 500 BCE. Each sign is associated with a specific set of characteristics and traits, and a person's zodiac sign is based on their birthday. These are the 12 traditionally recognized zodiac signs.

Below are their names and date/time frames:

- **Capricorn**: December 22–January 20
- **Aquarius:** January 21–February 19
- **Pisces**: February 20–March 20

- **Aries:** March 21–April 20
- **Taurus**: April 21–May 21
- **Gemini:** May 22–June 21
- **Cancer**: June 22–July 22
- **Leo**: July 23–August 23
- **Virgo**: August 24–September 23
- **Libra**: September 24–October 23
- **Scorpio**: October 24–November 22
- **Sagittarius**: November 23–December 21

Below is a list of the new zodiac horoscope dates as proposed by modern-day astronomers, courtesy of Bubala (2011):

- Capricorn: Jan. 20-Feb.16
- Aquarius: Feb. 16-March 11
- Pisces: March 11-April 18
- Aries: April 18-May 13
- Taurus: May 13-June 21
- Gemini: June 21-July 20
- Cancer: July 20-August 10
- Leo: August 10- Sept. 16
- Virgo: Sept. 16-Oct 30
- Libra: Oct. 30-Nov 23
- Scorpio: Nov. 23- Nov. 29
- Ophiuchus: Nov. 29-Dec. 17 (New sign)
- Sagittarius: Dec.17- Jan. 20

1.4 Overview of the characteristics of the Aries zodiac sign

Now, let us dive into the first exciting part of this journey: what makes you an Aries! We already know that you belong to this unique, pioneer zodiac sign if your birthday falls between March 21 and April 19. [As discussed above, note that some books or publications may list the Aries dates/time frames slightly differently from those listed here]. Aries is traditionally considered the first sign of the Zodiac and is described by astrologers as a constellation (group of stars) found between Pisces and Taurus and which appears in the night sky in the pattern of a ram (ram's horn). The Ram is, therefore, the zodiac symbol for Aries. The Aries' Ram is represented by various symbols in astrology. In modern astrology, the Aries' Ram is depicted by any of the following symbols: a ram's horns, a ram's head, a ram's torso, or the entire image of a ram. Here are some examples of common symbolic representations of the Aries zodiac sign:

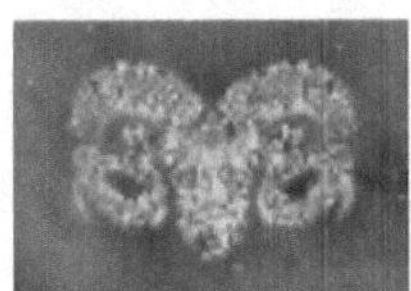

Why the Ram? Ancient mythology of various civilizations, including the Greeks and the Egyptians, associates the Ram with strength, boldness, determination, and creativity. One of the more widely accepted reasons for this symbolic representation of Aries is that the Ram represents the new beginnings, fertility, and prosperity that are hallmarks of the spring season, a time of renewal, re-growth, and re-purposing. The Aries constellation falls within the onset of the Spring months of March and April; therefore, it makes sense that it would be represented by a symbol associated with that season.

1.5 Significance of the Aries symbol: The Ram

"Aries" is the Latin word for "ram" (Mendillo, 2022). Its origin as the symbolic representation of the first zodiac sign is believed to be related to ancient Greek and Egyptian mythology. The Ram's horn is commonly associated with brutal physical strength. Think of how rams fight: headfirst, pushing forward, and literally "ramming" against their opponent. This characteristic is thought to confer the following attributes to individuals born within the Aries sign: courage, leadership, assertiveness, initiative, pioneering spirit, enthusiasm, determination, and action-oriented. Members of this sign have a reputation for being trailblazers who are often the first to try new things. They tend to have a proactive approach to life in general. They approach challenges head-on without hesitation, as symbolized by the "forward thrust" of the Ram's horns. They are very competitive by nature and demonstrate a direct and fearless attitude. Aries men and women are both brave and assertive, often the ones to take charge in relationships and careers.

1.6 Famous Aries Personalities

Many celebrity Aries are known for their larger-than-life personalities, leadership roles, and/or stubborn, headstrong personas. Take a look at some of them, courtesy of Cosmopolitan (2024):

- Elton John (March 25, 1947)
- Anya Taylor-Joy (April 16, 1996),
- Sarah Jessica Parker (March 25, 1965),
- Robert Downey, Jr (April 4, 1965),
- Keira Knightley (March 26, 1985),
- Victoria Beckham (April 17, 1974),
- Kourtney Kardashian (April 18, 1979),
- Mariah Carey (March 27),
- Lady Gaga (March 28, 1986),
- Reese Witherspoon (March 22, 1976)
- Emma Watson (April 15, 1990),
- America Ferrera (April 18, 1984),
- Lil Nas X (April 9, 1999),
- Kristen Stewart (April 9, 1990), and
- Halle Bailey (March 27, 2000).

Chapter 2

Elemental Insight: Which Element Rules You?

2.1 The zodiac elements and the signs they rule.

Have you ever wondered why you get along with certain personalities more than others? Or why you seem to attract the same type of partners in your love relationships? The answer to these questions most likely has much to do with your ruling zodiac element. The signs of the Zodiac System are ruled by four elements: fire, earth, air, and water. Each zodiac sign is ruled by one of the four elements, which means that each element rules (controls) three zodiac signs.

Below is the classification of the signs based on their ruling element:

- **Fire**: Aries, Leo, Sagittarius
- **Earth**: Taurus, Virgo, Capricorn

- **Air**: Gemini, Libra, Aquarius
- **Water**: Cancer, Pisces, Scorpio

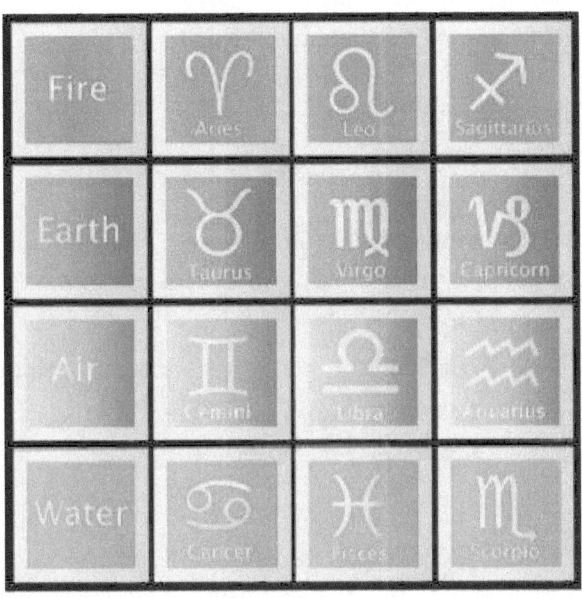

Together with the fundamental attributes associated with a person's sun sign and ruling planet, the four zodiac elements (fire, earth, air, and water) play a crucial role in molding personalities and predicting behaviors (Reed, 2024). These elements are the foundational influences determining the personality and characteristic behaviors associated with each of the twelve zodiac signs. They function by imparting unique qualities, channeling energies, influencing motivations, and predicting life approaches. In addition to being classified by elements, the twelve zodiac signs may also be classified based on how they express the energy they receive from their ruling element. The three classifications based on elemental quality/expression are **cardinal** elements, **fixed** elements, and **mutable** elements (Reed, 2024). The combination of elemental energy received plus elemental energy expression is manifested as part of the person's personality. Simply stated, each zodiac sign has its own unique way of expressing the energy it receives from its ruling element.

These two classification systems described above may be summarized as follows for the zodiac signs:

- **Fire** is passionate and fiery, Earth is practical and logical, **Air** is intellectual, and **Water** is emotional.
- **Cardinal** likes to get things started (Starters; Leaders), **Fixed** likes to sustain and maintain things (Equilibrium; Intellectuals), and **Mutable** likes to go with the flow (Adaptable; Pleasers).

Table 2.1 depicts a simplified version of the interconnected relationship between the zodiac signs, their ruling elements, their ruling planets, and their preferred method/quality of expression. The Fire Element rules the zodiac sign, Aries.

2.2 Aries as a fire sign

The three zodiac signs that are under the influence of the fire element are collectively known as the "Fire Signs," and this includes Aries, Leo, and Sagittarius. Fire signs are known for their energy, passion, enthusiasm, boldness, and courage. They tend to be adventurous and easily stand out from the crowd. That co-worker with a big personality who is often the first to volunteer to lead projects is likely either an Aries or a Leo in action. The classmate in your college science class who typically captivates the class with stories of new experiences and adventures and who usually can't wait to try the new chemistry experiment is likely a Sagittarius. These individuals appear to be imbued with boundless energy that propels them to be adventurous and immensely creative. They thrive when they are in action, and they relate pretty well with people, more so when they are the center of attention.

The Aries individual, in particular, being both a cardinal and a fire sign, tends to manifest the most intense version of these fiery elemental qualities. As you may recall, the cardinal individual initiates and tends to get things started. Similarly, the fire sign tends to be bold and enthusiastic. The combination of these A-type characteristics makes the Aries individual a strong personality in general. The passionate essence of the Fire element causes Aries to show a natural tendency to assume responsibility, to initiate and direct actions, to embrace challenges boldly, and to be fiercely independent. For the Aries, these attributes translate into an innate affinity for leadership and entrepreneurial positions. At times, Aries's impulsive and bold embrace of challenges galvanizes them into being trendsetters and pioneers in their field of expertise and, indeed, in various facets of life.

Table 2.1: Interplay of the ruling element, ruling planet, and expression quality/pattern for the 12 zodiac signs.

Sign	Zodiac Element	Ruling Planet	Quality
Aries	Fire	Mars	Cardinal
Taurus	Earth	Venus	Fixed
Gemini	Air	Mercury	Mutable
Cancer	Water	Moon	Cardinal
Leo	Fire	Sun	Fixed
Virgo	Earth	Mercury	Mutable
Libra	Air	Venus	Cardinal
Scorpio	Water	Pluto	Fixed
Sagittarius	Fire	Jupiter	Mutable
Capricorn	Earth	Saturn	Cardinal
Aquarius	Air	Uranus	Fixed
Pisces	Water	Neptune	Mutable

Chapter 3

Celestial Influences

3.1 Your ruling planet: Mars

In astrology, the location of the ruling planet (or ruling celestial body) is critical because it influences an individual's motivation, decision-making style, and approach to life in general. Mars is the ruling planet of those born within the time period of the zodiac sign Aries, which means that Mars is located explicitly within the Aries belt at the time of birth of these individuals. "Mars in Aries" manifests as a "planet of action" and is interpreted in Vedic astrology as a potent, powerful, and highly influential combination. How, you may ask? Mars is the planet of the god of war in ancient Greek mythology and, therefore, is associated with fearlessness, boldness, aggression, and passion. Similarly, the Aries' symbolic ram is associated with power/strength, courage, and determination. These two cardinal forces infuse the Aries's personality with a naturally strong sense of confidence, assertiveness, and enthusiasm. These individuals are energetic, proactive, ambitious, competitive, and passionate. They are resilient in the face of adversity and often make great leaders. The amplification of Mars' unbridled energy by the Aries' natural curiosity, sense of adventure, confidence, decisiveness, and enthusiasm makes these individuals readily embrace changes by acting decisively and quickly, contributing to their success in leadership roles. It is, therefore, no surprise that they tend to be drawn to careers that involve taking charge, initiating and leading projects, developing or trialing new ideas, or managing individuals and groups (teams). They thrive as business entrepreneurs, company executives, surgeons, attorneys, and law enforcement. In chapter four of this book, there will be further in-depth discussions about the characteristic strengths and challenges Aries individuals face.

3.2 The Sun's impact: Your core personality and ego

Core personality: In general, the Sun's influence on those born under any sign is to determine and shape their core personality and ego. The Sun is associated with an individual's self-identity, radiance, and confidence. The planet Mars rules Arians, and they tend to be assertive, full of life, and harbor an adventurous spirit. Therefore, when the Sun's vibrant warmth fuels their ego, they demonstrate an intrinsic desire for independence, individuality, leadership, and assertiveness. These solar-driven Aries personas are naturally inclined to take charge, lead, express their opinions, and take chances. They harness the fiery and vibrant solar energy to transform themselves into self-driven, dynamic personalities. They are most of the "go-getters" of this world.

Ego: The Sun's warmth stimulates the Arian personality to crave attention, recognition, and even adulation. It also positions them to bask in the limelight and propels them to rise to challenges. Their sun-charged ego/persona encourages Aries to take the initiative and try new things, often becoming pioneers and trailblazers in their field of pursuit.

3.3 The Moon's role: Your emotions and inner self

The Moon's presence in Aries introduces an emotional twist into the mix of Aries characteristics. The Moon in Aries introduces passion, emotion, impulsivity, bluntness/directness, volatility, high energy, and a competitive spirit into the Aries personality. When this is combined with the bold, assertive, proactive, ambitious, and supercharged confidence that was imbued in these individuals by their ruling element (fire) and by the influence of the sun and their ruling planet (Mars), the result is an amplification of these traits into emotional intensity, passionate energy, and vibrant enthusiasm. This lunar placement also encourages the Aries to be more intuitive, instinctual, and spontaneous in their responses to life and events rather than rational and contemplative. From a positive perspective, this reactionary approach to life and events causes Aries to be fun, adventurous, and creative. It also causes them to be very direct and honest, often coming across as unapologetically blunt. You can probably think of a friend or coworker whose personality resembles this description. On the negative side, however, they may be impulsive, reckless, emotionally labile, quick-tempered, and easily frustrated, as evidenced by characteristic passionate outbursts. Emotional awareness and patience are two personality traits that Aries should seek and acquire to balance the downside of this Moon-in-Aries effect.

At this point, it is pertinent to mention that the Moon Phase at birth also plays a role in determining which aspect of the Moon-in-Aries effect is amplified versus subdued. For instance, those Aries individuals born during a waxing moon may demonstrate increased confidence and a desire for new experiences. They may also exhibit heightened adaptability and thrive in dynamic environments. [A **waxing moon** is a growing/increasing moon that enlarges in size each night as it moves towards the full moon stage).

Conversely, the Aries born during a waning moon may tend to be more subdued. They might experience more periods of introspection or a tempering of their fiery nature with periods of reflection and emotional depth. This means that although their inherent tendency to be bold, confident, assertive, independent, and competitive remains central to their identity, the waning moon's energy could introduce moments of caution and hesitation, prompting them to evaluate their risks more carefully. [A **waning moon** occurs after a full moon as it gradually decreases in size until the next new moon occurs].

Chapter 4

Astrological Personality Prediction:

What Makes You Unique?

4.1 Aries: Characteristics and strengths

So far in this discussion, we have determined that the overall personality presented by any individual is the result of the interplay between several astrological factors, such as the elemental ruler of the individual's primary zodiac sign and the positions of the sun, moon, and stars relative to the cosmic world and relative to each other. This section utilizes the above knowledge to predict the Aries personality, emphasizing this pace-setting zodiac entity's positive characteristics and strength.

Every individual's personality is the product of the layering of several factors within their birth chart, prominent of which are the Sun, the Moon, and the Ascendant (aka ruling planet). This combination of Sun, Moon, and Ascendant makes each individual unique.

The Sun: Your sun sign is generally called the "zodiac sign" or "star sign." The "Sun Sign" corresponds to the position/location of the sun at the time of your birth. For instance, the sun's position between March 21st and April 19th is in the Aries constellation of stars. The sun sign reveals the soul pathway of the individual. It is the expression of the personal ego. It is your true self.

The Moon: The moon sign oversees and predicts an individual's emotions and instinctual approach to life. It depicts how you nurture yourself. It represents the expectations that run (control) the subconscious self.

The Ascendant: The Ascendant is the sign rising over the eastern horizon at the specific time of birth (also called "Ascendant Rising"). Each Ascendant sign is believed to be ruled by a planet or "god/goddess" who oversaw a person's birth and governed the course of their entire life. For example, Planet Mars rules an Aries ascendant, whereas Planet Saturn rules a Capricornian ascendant. The Ascendant sign is described as "the mask" that you present to the world to hide your true self. It is your **alter ego**, the "face" or image that you present to the world as you. When people perceive you differently from who you truly are, this is due to the Ascendant effect. I am sure we have seen many instances whereby people perceive an individual differently in different areas of their lives. They may be the perfect dad, husband, and likable community leader in their home environment, but then they could be described as cold and unfriendly at their workplace. It is important to note that whenever the Sun sign does not fit a person's personality or character, you will find that their Moon or Ascendant sign is predominant.

The Aries's strength of character comes from the combined positive influences from Mars (their ruling planet or Ascendant), the Sun, and the Moon. Below is a recap of these personality strengths:

- **Bold, Fearless, Direct, Driven, Ambitious, and Independent**: Mars, the ruling planet for Aries, is known as the "action planet," so it is no surprise that individuals born under the Aries zodiac sign tend to manifest personality features that are aligned with vitality, adventure, enthusiasm, and individualism.

- **Energetic, Radiant, Confident, and Competitive**: The Sun-in-Mars is a predominant force that propels Aries to exude energy, power, and influence. Their energy is described as "vibrant". People find them exciting and are attracted to them naturally. As an Aries, you are a people person for the most part. You enjoy being recognized, respected, and the center of attention. You thrive on people's optimistic view of you as a person and as a professional. Challenges and competition stimulate you. You are adventurous and creative.

- **Impulsive and passionate with a vigorous emotional intensity**: With the Moon in Aries, you are fueled by a passionate view and commitment to what you believe in, sometimes to the point of being headstrong. Your high energy and solid emotional intensity create a need for you to be active and engaged most of the time. Your impulsive nature from your moon's influence stimulates your creative side.

- **Enthusiasm and optimism**: The enthusiasm and optimism with which Aries approaches life's events and tasks is infectious and attractive. This makes them very likable and a considerable asset for the team during demanding tasks.
- **Natural leadership qualities**: You can always count on Aries to assume the leadership role for projects and succeed in most instances.
- **Resilience, determination, and ambition**: When their solar (sun) and lunar (moon) energies are appropriately harnessed, Aries can channel these energies into resilience, determination, and focused ambition in whatever they pursue while also cultivating and maintaining healthy emotional connections with the people around them.

4.2 Aries: Common challenges and how to overcome them

Although the challenges discussed here are viewed as the "dark side" of their personality, my recommendation is that they should not be viewed as unfavorable but rather as challenges that require refinement and fine-tuning to create the ultimate, wholesome, and balanced Aries life. Here are some common challenges that Aries individuals may face:

- **Impatience**: The Aries-Sun-inspired dominant, confident, and competitive nature of the Aries personality causes them to struggle with seeing another person's point of view because they believe they are always right. Their high energy and impatience can also manifest physically because the Aries person may struggle to wait their turn or wait for team members to catch up on a project. It would not be unusual for them to have difficulty simply waiting for their spouse or family member to get ready for an outing.

- **Quick temper (anger issues):** Anger (temper) issues are considered a significant weakness for Aries of both sexes. The combined influences of the fiery red planet (Mars) and the Moon in Aries can be pretty powerful, especially for those Aries born during a waxing moon. If not managed appropriately, their tendency to have emotional outbursts can be disruptive personally and damaging professionally. Their feelings are intense and direct, which results in a hot temper. Also, because the Aries are action-oriented by nature, there is a high probability that they will take immediate action while in that highly emotional state. It is thought that the Aries' short temper lies at the heart of most of their personality flaws. Interestingly, although Aries may be quick to anger, they do not hold grudges like the Scorpios do.
- **Depression:** Depression is the result of reversed anger issues and occurs when the Aries individual bottles up their anger without any outlet for it. As Hall (2014) describes it, "For the Aries, depression is anger turned inward."
- **Restlessness**: Due to their high energy, Aries individuals may quickly get bored and seek additional

stimulation to focus their energy. This is an essential factor to consider in a relationship with an Aries individual.

- **Impulsiveness (Reactionary)**: The impulsive nature of the Aries may often result in reactionary responses to people and events. They may not necessarily think or consider consequences before acting.

- **Stubborn and Egotistical**: Other descriptors ascribed to Aries in this category of challenges are stubborn, headstrong, willful, egotistical, unapologetic, intimidating, and like to have their way. In general, people born into the Aries zodiac sign have difficulty accepting that they are wrong and can be perceived as unapologetic and intimidating.

- **Bluntness (Directness)**: Most Aries are thick-skinned and have no filter for their speech, which may come across as mean, harsh, or cruel. Sometimes, the other person perceives their open emotions and brutal honesty as blunt or insensitive. This may create friction and misunderstanding personally and professionally.

It is essential to understand that these "dark" attributes discussed above often result from an improperly channeled positive trait. For example, misuse of Aries's positive, assertive nature will manifest negatively as pushy, aggressive, or combative. Similarly, Aries' dominant personality traits (boldness, energy, and fearlessness) could manifest as headstrong, egotistical, or arrogant if not appropriately managed.

For this reason, it is crucial that Aries individuals utilize the self-care tools discussed in Chapter Five to enhance their positive personality traits and thus create an optimized and fulfilling lifestyle for themselves.

How to manage common Aries challenges naturally.

As stated above, most of the challenging aspects of Aries' personality are actually not necessarily negative attributes but rather excessive or improperly managed positive traits. Learning to manage or control these behavioral traits is usually not a quick fix. There is no standard recipe that solves the problem for every Aries because each Aries is a unique and complex mix of traits. The process is usually ongoing, involving testing what works best for you in the long term. Various non-pharmacological (non-medicinal) tools can be utilized to achieve this. These are listed below:

- Breathing exercises
- Meditative practices, such as mindful meditation, affirmative chants, meditative counting, yoga,
- Chakra healing, which involves the manipulation and balancing of the human subtle energies (chakra)
- Gem/Crystal therapy, which involves the channeling of energies by the use of crystals and gemstones
- Aromatherapy, including the use of herbs and essential oils
- Sound therapy
- Light therapy
- Reiki, a type of hands-on spiritual healing
- Acupuncture, Tai Chi, Shiatsu, and other traditional Chinese healing practices

- High-energy hobbies such as gym workouts, cycling, and other creative pursuits serve as healthy outlets for positively channeling excess energy.

Most of the above-listed techniques and tools have been practiced and utilized respectively by ancient and diverse cultures worldwide for thousands of years, including the ancient Babylonians, Egyptians, Persians, Greeks, Tibetans, Chinese, Indians, and South American Mayans. This book will focus mainly on the first four listed (breathing exercises, meditative practices, chakra healing, and gemstone/crystal therapy). These will be briefly discussed in this section and in more detail in subsequent chapters.

Below are some ways these tools may be used to manage Aries' challenging traits.

- Anger issues, impulsivity, and restlessness can be effectively managed with breathing exercises (box breathing, deep breathing). These exercises work by slowing the heart rate, maintaining vital signs within baseline limits, and eliminating other stress symptoms associated with the physiological changes accompanying a rising temper.
- Impulsivity, restlessness, and impatience can be effectively managed using various meditative techniques (mindfulness meditation, meditative counting, and so on). The efficacy of meditative practices lies in the principle of conscious and intentional slowing and redirection/channeling of one's thoughts and thought processes, thereby slowing

and redirecting responses to events. Once learned and mastered, meditative practices would help the Aries to stop and think before speaking or acting. In other words, they will be less impulsive, impatient, and reactionary, and instead, they will make better choices and become more considerate of other people's feelings.

- Nurturing and maintaining balance in the seven chakras would effectively address all of the challenges above because a well-nurtured and balanced chakra results in a healthy balance of the self, ego, and emotion.

- Using Aries-compatible gemstones and crystals to eliminate negative energies and to attract, retain, and properly align your positive energies will eliminate any traits or challenges originating from energy misalignment.

- Aromatherapy using Aries-compatible herbs and essential oils is effective for relaxation and stress relief. Various cultures and civilizations have used this practice for years.

These tools can be used alone but typically as combinations to either upregulate positive traits or downregulate and disperse challenging (negative) attributes. As we progress in subsequent chapters of this book, we will explore how these tools can be aligned to create an optimal daily routine for members of this fascinating zodiac sign, Aries.

Important to Know

It is necessary to emphasize at this point that no one Aries individual possesses all the characteristics described above. The totality of a person's personality and character is much more complex than just the zodiac sign to which they belong. Instead, it is also determined by other factors such as genetics, upbringing, environment, and social factors. Therefore, it is absolutely normal to find two Aries who do not have the same personality. For example, an Aries individual may manifest more quick-thinking, initiative, and assertive skills and be less bold, risk-taking, and adventurous than another Aries who may be highly energetic, boldly ambitious, and wildly impulsive. Both are still Aries and would likely be good leaders, but they would have different approaches.

Part Two

Self-Care

"Mysticism is not an escape from reality. It is the art of anchoring in reality."

— Swami Sivananda

"People can live completely without astrology... if they do not care about knowing who they are."

— Liz Greene

Chapter 5

Essential Self-Care Tools for the Aries

5.1 Alternative & Meditative Practices and Their Roles in Self-Care

Recently, there has been increased interest in meditative practices such as yoga, mindfulness meditation, affirmative mantras, and channeling energies (chakra healing, crystal healing, and reiki). In fact, the words "mindful meditation" and "chakras" have become catchphrases in popular culture these days. This uptick in interest in meditative practices has led to more scientific research investigating the claims of health benefits associated with these esoteric practices to possibly incorporate them into traditional medicine.

Black & Slavich (2016) conducted a peer-reviewed randomized control trial evaluating whether any relationship exists between mindful meditation and the body's immune system. Their findings suggest that mindful meditation may have potentially beneficial effects on specific inflammatory markers in the body and on cell-mediated immunity and biological aging. However, they recommend further replication studies and research based on the limitations of their work. They also noted that their research data suggested that the effects of mindful meditation may be *salutogenic* for the immune system but pointed out that additional studies are needed to examine these effects.

Salutogenesis

Now, let us explore the concept of salutogenesis for a little bit. What is salutogenesis? The Merriam-Webster dictionary of the English language defines salutogenesis as an approach to human health that examines the factors contributing to promoting and maintaining physical and mental well-being rather than disease. Salutogenesis is a health theory credited to Israeli-American medical sociologist Aaron Antonovsky (1979) in his renowned book titled *Health, Stress, and Coping*, where he proposed that although health and disease (illness) are two sides of the same complex continuum, placing the focus and emphasis on assets, strengths, and motivation as a way to maintain and improve health is more beneficial and enduring than focusing on the treatment of disease (Mittelmark & Bauer, 2016). He called his theory "salutogenesis". Simply stated, salutogenesis focuses on those influences and factors that support health rather than those that cause disease. Over time, this theory has been applied in other specialties outside of medicine, based on the generally accepted salutogenic principle that life experiences help modify and re-purpose one's sense of global coherence (global orientation), that is, one's sense of meaning/comprehension/understanding of the world around us.

So, how does salutogenesis relate to self-care tools? Based on the definitions explained above, salutogenesis supports using non-traditional interventions and tools, such as meditative practices, for health promotion and maintenance instead of treating illnesses resulting from an absence of self-care using traditionally accepted pharmacological methods (medications).

Let's investigate and understand each of the meditative practices before delving into how the Aries can utilize them for self-care.

5.2 Relaxation Techniques: Mindfulness Meditation and Breathwork

We will discuss the two most commonly used relaxation techniques: Mindfulness Meditation and Breathing Exercises (Breathwork)

A. Mindfulness Meditation

What comes to mind when you hear or think of "mindfulness meditation"? I posed this question to random individuals during the research process for writing this book. Based on the responses I received, most people immediately think of yoga meditation poses when they hear "meditation" or "mindfulness meditation." However, in reality, mindfulness meditation is more than assuming the classic lotus position or clasping the hands together in a cross-legged seated position with the eyes closed. There is more involvement of the mind (the will) and the intention in this process than typically imagined. Mindfulness is described as being wholly present in the moment in an accepting and non-judgmental manner. The American Psychological Association defines mindfulness meditation as training the mind and attention to achieve a mental and physiologic state of calm, concentration, and positive emotions (American Psychological Association 2019). The technique derives from the combination of two concepts:

- the concept of mindfulness (whereby the person remains in the present moment because they are fully aware of their surroundings and what is going on around them while also remaining connected to their inner thought and feelings); and
- the concept of meditation (whereby the person can explore the inner workings of their mind by fully experiencing different sensations associated with everyday actions such as breathing, smelling, inhaling, or listening). (Brenan, 2021).

Mindfulness meditation involves getting into the subconscious mind (that is, getting into your own head) and calming it down to create a safe, open space where you can do anything you want. (Woodward, 2023). Properly executing mindfulness meditation means suspending any underlying biases or judgments and applying intention to adopt an attitude of openness and kindness (Brennan, 2021). Mindfulness meditation teaches how to subdue one's unconscious reactions and instead apply objectivity in analyzing thoughts and emotions. The three qualities required to practice mindfulness meditation effectively are wakefulness, intention, and mental discipline (Brennan, 2021).

Even though its popularity as a psychological and mental health intervention has just recently exploded, mindfulness has existed and been practiced for centuries. Its origins can be traced back to the meditative practices of the far eastern Buddhist and Indian Hindu religions. Its recent popularity (especially in popular culture) has led to many systematic reviews and meta-analysis research efforts to determine its efficacy and potential benefits as a medically approved intervention. One of the many high-quality research studies conducted on mindfulness meditation is a meta-analysis of a review of mindfulness-based therapy (MBT) conducted in 2013 by Khoury et al. Their study results showed that MBT is moderately effective in pre- and post-study samples compared to other active treatments (including psychoeducation and supportive therapy). After reviewing over 200 studies of mindfulness among healthy people, researchers concluded that mindfulness-based therapy (MBT) was significantly effective in reducing stress, anxiety, and depression. Some of the most promising research findings were seen in people suffering from depression. Other specific health problems that have benefited from mindfulness meditation are pain, high blood pressure, smoking, and addiction. Other similar studies show that mindfulness meditation may boost the immune system and shorten the recovery time for colds and flu (APA, 2019).

How does mindfulness work?

You may wonder how the seemingly innocuous action of merely channeling your thoughts and feelings produces so many positive outcomes throughout the body. Researchers believe the benefits of mindfulness are related to its ability to dial down the body's response to stress. Research psychologists propose that mindfulness lowers the body's stress response through its ability to trigger a down-regulation of the stress response mechanism. (APA, 2019). Chronic stress is associated with many health problems because it triggers the persistence of stress hormones in the bloodstream and weakens the body's immune system. Based on research evidence, psychologists demonstrated that mindfulness works by modifying the brain structure and activity in the two stress pathways in the brain that are associated with attention and emotion regulation. Their research data produced substantial evidence to show that people who received mindfulness-based cognitive therapy (MBCT) were less likely to produce reactionary responses to negative thoughts during times of stress. The data also showed that moderate evidence supports the theory that people who participated in mindfulness-based stress reduction (MBSR) and mindfulness-based cognitive therapy (MBCT) were more likely to focus on the present time and less likely to worry or dwell on negative thoughts or experiences repeatedly.

Benefits of mindfulness meditation

Based on the discussion above, here are some of the benefits that have been ascribed to mindfulness meditation:

- Reduction of relapse in people previously diagnosed with major depression.
- Pain, fatigue, and stress reduction in people with chronic pain.

- Mindfulness meditation is credited with boosting the immune system. This is evidenced by quicker recovery from cold and the flu in the research subjects tested.

Mindfulness meditation classes are available across various settings, including clinics, hospitals, gyms, yoga centers, community recreation centers, and fitness centers. Using a therapist trained in MBSR or MBCT is highly recommended because these interventions yielded evidence of the most benefits from the research studies (APA, 2019).

A simple mindful meditation exercise

Remember that although it may take you a little while to get used to mindfulness meditation and make it part of your regular daily routine, it is worth the effort because, with patience and practice, it could become a powerful tool for relieving stress and improving your well-being as an Aries. With this in mind, here is a simple mindful meditation exercise to get you started.

- **Find a quiet space**: Begin by finding a quiet and comfortable space that is free from distractions.
- **Assume a comfortable position**: Assume the most comfortable position for you. This may be sitting or lying down; it does not really matter which one you choose. For example, you may sit comfortably in a chair or on the floor or lie down on a mat on your back or side on the floor. Once you are comfortably positioned, keep your back straight, hands resting on your lap, and close your eyes (if

seated), or keep your back straight and close your eyes (if lying down).

- **Relax and free your mind**: With eyes closed, consciously relax every muscle in your body and free your mind of all thoughts. You can achieve this by imagining every muscle tension as a weight dropping off your body and leaving it limp and light. Similarly, you can imagine intrusive thoughts as wisps of smoke or puffs of air that gently float out and away from your body

- **Focus on your breath**: Start by taking a few (three to five) deep breaths, inhaling each breath slowly through your nose and exhaling through your mouth. After the fifth breath, allow your breathing depth and pattern to return to its natural rhythm while paying attention to each inhale and exhale.

- **Notice sensations**: As you breathe, consciously notice how the air feels as it enters your nose, passes through your airways, fills your lungs, and leaves your body. Feel the rise and fall of your chest or abdomen with each breath you take.

- **Observe your thoughts**: As you continue to breathe and feel the sensations of each breath, if any thoughts or distractions arise, recognize and allow them to pass through without judgment. Then gently guide your focus back to your breathing. Continue allowing any stray thoughts to pass through without lingering, like clouds in the sky.

- **Stay in the present**: Continue to focus on your breath for about 5–10 minutes. If your mind wanders, simply and gently return your focus to the breath,

always keeping your attention on the present
moment.

- **End slowly**: When you are ready to end the
  exercise, slowly and gently guide your awareness back
  to your surroundings, beginning from your center to
  your extremities. To end, wiggle your fingers and
  toes, open your eyes, and take a moment before
  getting up.

Congratulations! You have just completed your first mindful meditation exercise! The above routine is the simplest form of mindfulness meditation. Did you notice that it is closely interwoven with breathing exercises? Most mindfulness meditation exercises involve an element of breathing (breathwork) exercise. Therefore, it is difficult to separate one from the other completely. The simple breathing pattern utilized in this exercise is called "focused breathing" or "conscious breathing." As a beginner, it will likely take you a little longer to achieve a state of complete relaxation. However, with practice, this will become easier and come naturally, and you will learn to prolong the relaxed state and even add more complex exercises to your routine.

B. Breathing Exercises (Breathwork)

What is Breathwork? Breathwork involves using various breathing techniques to intentionally control, channel, and focus the breathing rate, quality, and pattern to calm the body and the mind (*Breathwork for Beginners*, 2024). It is a medically recognized and accepted stress management technique used in Complementary and Alternative Medicine (CAM).

Principle underlying breathwork

Breathwork helps calm the mind and body to combat stress by reversing the physiological symptoms associated with the *fight-or-flight* stress response of the human body. The fight-or-flight response is the sympathetic nervous system's (SNS) response to danger or severe (life-threatening) situations, during which there is a surge of stress hormones like adrenaline and cortisol. This stress response was designed by nature to be a temporary response to an uncommon event or situation. It was not meant to be a permanent or prolonged state of the body due to the harm caused by prolonged stress hormones in the body/blood. Unfortunately, in today's modern world, humans are prone to daily (chronic) stressors that keep the body in a permanently stressed state. The result is a myriad of medical and mental health conditions, including cardiovascular disease (high blood pressure, stroke, heart attack, heart disease); endocrine imbalances and diseases (glucose intolerance, diabetes, obesity); Gastrointestinal disease conditions (ulcers, GERD, gastritis, irritable bowel syndrome, and irritable bowel disease); dermatological conditions involving the skin and hair (acne, hair loss, eczema, psoriasis); psychological and mental health conditions (anxiety, depression, insomnia, substance abuse, personality and social disorders); and so on. Breathwork reverses this chronic stress state by activating the body's parasympathetic nervous system (PNS), also known as the "rest-and-digest" system, which is responsible for relaxing the body after exposure to stress or danger. Breathwork achieves this de-escalation and de-stressing process by intentionally slowing and controlling the breathing pattern and rate, thereby controlling oxygen delivery to various body parts. The overall result is a slowing of respiratory and heart rates, lowering blood pressure, and reversing the need for adrenaline and cortisol release into the blood.

Breathwork has been practiced for thousands of years by many civilizations and is linked to Eastern medicine practices, including Ayurveda and traditional Chinese and Tibetan medicine. Breathwork has its roots in the esoteric practices of yoga and Eastern meditation. There are several previous and ongoing valuable research work on breathwork. One such research effort was a meta-analysis of several randomized controlled trials conducted by Fincham et al. (2023). This meta-analysis summarized that analysis of the results indicated that there was a statistically significant positive effect of breathwork on self-reported (subjective) stress, anxiety, and depression by the test subjects compared to non-breathwork conditions in the control subjects. Fincham et al. recommended further research in this area based on these promising results.

Benefits of breathwork

Scientific research on breathwork is ongoing and promising (as discussed above) and has shown the following potential health benefits:

- Increased oxygenation of body organs
- Alkalization of the blood pH
- Anti-inflammatory effects
- Mood-elevating effects
- Wound healing benefits

- Stress reduction through calming of the central nervous system by deepened relaxation
- Promote quality sleep/rest

Some types and techniques of breathwork

Below is a list of common breathwork types and techniques. We will briefly examine some of them and when to use them.

- Focused (Conscious) breathing
- Diaphragmatic (abdominal) breathing
- Pursed lip breathing
- Alternate nostril breathing
- Box breathing
- 4-7-8 breathing
- Five-Finger breathing
- Holotropic breathwork
- Lion's breath technique
- Bumblebee breath
- Breathwork meditation (Meditative breathwork or Meditative breathing)

Focused (Conscious) Breathing

As the name implies, focused breathing involves a conscious/intentional slowing down of the breath while paying attention to each breath and how the body feels. It is one of the most accessible and most commonly used breathing techniques for managing stress, anger, anxiety, and panic attacks. It is often combined with meditation in breathwork meditation (see the section on breathwork meditation for a simple description of focused breathing.

Diaphragmatic (abdominal) breathing

Diaphragmatic breathing involves breathing from the diaphragm (abdomen) rather than the chest. The diaphragm (lower part of the lungs) is engaged in this breathing technique, which results in deep breaths.

A simple diaphragmatic breathing exercise:

- While in a relaxed position, place one hand on the chest and the other hand on the abdomen.
- Breathe in slowly and deeply (inhale) without engaging the chest but allowing the diaphragm (abdomen) to rise and expand fully.
- Then breathe out slowly (exhale) while contracting the abdomen.

After complete exhalation, pause and hold your breath for a few seconds, then repeat the above process as needed until you are calm. This technique slows down the breathing rate. Using imagery for inhaling and exhaling helps achieve a slow and steady rhythm. The diaphragmatic breathwork technique is also often incorporated with meditation.

Pursed lip breathing

Pursed lip breathing involves breathing in through the nostrils and breathing out through pursed lips. It is considered an excellent tool for slowing breathing and reducing stress. It may benefit people with chronic lung conditions such as reactive airway disease, asthma, COPD, and cystic fibrosis. A simple pursed lip breathing exercise is as follows:

- Breathe in (inhale) slowly through your nose.
- Pucker (pout) your lips as if you are going to whistle or blow out a candle.
- Breathe out (exhale) slowly through your pursed lips while prolonging the exhalation time to be at least twice as long as the inhalation time.

You may repeat this as often as necessary to achieve your goal, which could be relaxation, bringing down your heart rate to manage anger or fear, or slowing down your breathing rate to address anxiety.

Alternate nostril breathing

The Alternate Nostril Breathing technique involves breathing through one nostril while covering the other and then alternating the nostrils on each inhale and exhale.

Box breathing

Box breathing involves inhaling for 4 seconds, followed by breath-holding for 4 seconds, exhaling for 4 seconds, and finally breath-holding again for 4 seconds to complete one cycle. Depending on the end goal, this may be repeated multiple times.

<u>Practice</u>:

Let us practice box breathing in detail since it is frequently used for various scenarios, including relaxation, stress reduction, mindfulness meditation, etc.

Step 1. Breathe OUT slowly, expelling all the air from your lungs.

Step 2. Breathe IN slowly through your nostrils while silently counting from one to four. Notice how the air slowly flows through your air passages and fills your lungs and belly.

Step 3. HOLD your breath now for a count of four.

Step 4. EXHALE slowly for another count of four.

Step 5. HOLD your breath again for a count of four to complete one cycle of box breathing.

Each complete box breathing cycle should be "IN-HOLD-OUT-HOLD,"

You may repeat the cycle for up to five rounds or as desired.

4-7-8 breathing

Each cycle of the 4-7-8 breathing exercise involves inhaling for four (4) seconds through the nose, followed by breath-holding for seven (7) seconds and then exhaling through the mouth for eight (8) seconds. This is repeated several times. This can be repeated for several cycles.

<u>Practice</u>:

Step 1. Breathe in (INHALE) through your **nostrils** for a count of four (4).

Step 2. HOLD your breath for a count of seven (7).

Step 3. EXHALE fully through your mouth in a whooshing sound for a count of eight (8).

4-7-8 breathing is an effective mechanism for managing anxiety attacks.

Five-finger breathing

Five-finger breathing is a simple technique in which you breathe in and out, following a pattern as you trace each of your five fingers up and down. It is believed to slow the heart rate (which diffuses anger and anxiety), balance the body, and provide sensory feedback to the brain.

Holotropic breathwork

Holotropic breathwork is a controlled breathing technique that involves rapid and even breathing. It is believed to induce an altered state of consciousness during which the participant achieves enlightenment and personal empowerment that can be channeled into self-healing. (Grof, n.d.). The experience has been described as a more intense form of meditation. The underlying cornerstone for holotropic breathwork is that each individual has an inner healing intelligence and impulse.

Lion's breath technique

The Lion's breathwork technique involves inhaling deeply through your nose for a few counts followed by a forceful exhalation through the mouth while sticking out your tongue and making a 'haaaa' sound," In yoga, this breathwork technique goes together with the "roaring lion pose," also known as simhasana.

Bumblebee breathing

This is also called "Bhramari Pranayama" breathing which involves breathing in deeply and making a high-pitched humming sound that mimics the buzzing of a bee during exhalation. This technique helps to reduce stress, anxiety, and tension, promote relaxation and inner peace, and improve concentration. It is considered a very useful tool for centering the mind and body.

Breathwork meditation

Breathwork meditation refers to any technique that combines breathing exercises with mindfulness. Combining breathwork with meditation allows you to potentially reap the benefits of both techniques. Many people use breathwork meditation to deepen relaxation, improve focus, and unwind before bedtime. They also use breathwork meditation to improve their mental, emotional, and physical well-being (Healthline, 2023). Any breathwork exercise pattern can be combined with meditation, but the most commonly used are focused (conscious) breathing, diaphragmatic (abdominal) breathing, and box breathing.

General Tips for Breathwork Meditation Exercises

The first thing to remember is that, like every other skill, breathwork meditation requires patience and time and will become easier with regular practice.

Here are some valuable tips to boost your breathwork meditation experience:

- Set aside time to practice every day or regularly at the very least.
- Create a quiet space where you can practice without distractions or interruptions.
- Feel free to try out different techniques to figure out which one works best for you.

- Suppose you are not confident trying it out alone. In that case you can search YouTube, Audible, Spotify, and various mindfulness apps for guided breathwork meditation videos and audio, in which a guide leads you through the exercise.
- You also have the option to search online for a certified breathwork practitioner to assist you in beginning and establishing a routine.

Every individual is different and, therefore, will have variable experiences with breathwork meditation. If, after a reasonable period of regular practice, you still cannot relax during breathwork meditation or you tend to be overly anxious during the exercise, this may indicate that this relaxation technique is not for you. In that case, you may try other mindful meditation techniques that do not involve breathwork.

A simple breathing meditation exercise

Please refer to the section "A simple mindful meditation exercise" to review the steps for conducting a simple breathing meditation exercise.

5.3 Aromatherapy

Aromatherapy is the use of fragrant (aromatic) plant extracts and essential oils for therapeutic (healing) purposes and to promote a sense of relaxation and well-being using various carrier vehicles (lotions, massage oils, diffusers, candles) and various methods (steam inhalation, massage, etc.). Aromatherapy is accepted in modern medicine as a complementary and alternative medicine (CAM) therapy. The PDQ

Cancer Information Summaries (2005) describes aromatherapy as therapeutically using aromatic extracts (essential oils) from plants, flowers, herbs, or trees to improve physical, emotional, psychological, and spiritual well-being. These plant/herbal extracts are often concentrated volatile oils that must be diluted in high-quality carrier agents to produce essential oils that may be used as inhalation or topical treatment agents. Note that many reputable authorities recommend that aromatherapy should never be administered through the mouth (ingestion) to avoid possible toxicity ((PDQ et al. Editorial Board, 2005). Animal studies and human clinical trials have investigated aromatherapy extensively and confirmed the following potential uses:

- Antibacterial effects
- Anti-inflammatory effects
- Sedative effects
- Stimulant effects
- Analgesic effects
- Treatment of stress and anxiety (demonstrated by human clinical trials)
- Upregulation of the immune system
- Positive effects on behaviors

Furthermore, several human clinical trials have been published demonstrating aromatherapy's benefits for cancer patients in the areas listed above. The underlying theory explaining the effects of aromatherapy is that the chemical components in the essential oil bind to receptors in the olfactory bulb (found in the nasal cavity just beneath the brain) and, from there, send messages to the brain that impact the brain's emotional center (also known as the limbic system).

Aromatherapy for Aries

Aromatherapy for those born under the Aries sign targets either of two pathways: restoration versus soothing.

1. **Aromatherapy for restoring energy**: Aries individuals who are physically and mentally depleted (exhausted) require specific essential oils to restore their innate energy. The best essential oils for Aries in this category are **_"warm essential oils."_** These include rosemary, black pepper, and ginger. The signature warm essential oil for Aries is Rosemary.

2. **Aromatherapy for calming/soothing energy**: Conversely, stressed Aries will benefit immensely from "soothing essential oils," specifically Bergamot, German chamomile, Roman chamomile, and Geranium. Bergamot is the signature soothing essential oil for Aries.

Aromatherapy is one of my favorite self-care regimens because it is so easy to use. Remember that the purpose of these oils is to restore the energy balance to baseline. I recommend setting up your aromatherapy before you begin your self-care meditation and allowing time for the restoring or soothing scents to reset your energy level so that you will be in an optimal mental state for the best results from your meditation.

of the diluted oil to a small skin area before applying it to a large skin surface.

Don'ts:

3. Avoid drinking or ingesting aromatherapy oil by mouth: You should never take essential oils by mouth (ingestion) without the specific directions of a trained and qualified CAM specialist. Do not add drops of aromatherapy oil to tea, coffee, or water for drinking.
4. Never apply essential oil directly to the body from the bottle. Some are corrosive.
5. Avoid using or storing essential oils near open flames to avoid starting a fire. Essential oils are highly flammable volatile liquids. This means they can easily catch fire when exposed to a flame.
6. Pregnant and breastfeeding women should avoid using aromatherapy oil without a doctor's supervision to avoid potential toxicity to the baby.
7. Keep aromatherapy (essential) oils away from children and pets because large amounts can be toxic when ingested.

Remember: Although derived from nature, aromatherapy/essential oils are powerful substances that could be harmful if not used properly.

Let's look at the two signature essential oils for members of the Aries zodiac sign: Rosemary (signature warm essential oil) and Bergamot (signature calming/soothing essential oil).

Rosemary (*Rosmarinus officinalis*):

- Both soothing and uplifting effects; Good for reversing emotional burnout
- Eases stress (soothing effect) and uplifts mood (restorative effect) to prevent emotional burnout. (Ilana, 2021).

Bergamot oil (citrus bergamia):

- Extracted from fresh bergamot orange fruit
- Citrus scent with a fresh floral note that is similar to the smell of sweet orange peel oil or lemon/lime oil.
- Used to relieve stress and anxiety, increase mental alertness, reduce joint pain and other inflammatory conditions, and facilitate wound healing (Healthline, 2018).
- May also be used for grounding (centering) the mind.

A popular way of using essential oils and herb extracts is by mixing a selection of oils into a blend. Essential oil blends tailored for Aries may include the two signature essential oils (rosemary, bergamot) plus a variety of Aries-compatible oils such as: black pepper, black spruce, fragonia, frankincense, lemon, and Roman chamomile. Others include rose oil, peppermint oil, geranium oil, patchouli, and frankincense oil. These blends may be prepared for use in diffusers, scented roll-ons, spritzes, air freshener sprays, etc. Most aromatherapy practitioners and reputable stores will advise customers on which combination of oils or herbs to blend (mix) that matches their personality.

Below is a brief description and primary uses of popular essential oils for preparing blends for Aries individuals.

- **Rose oil**: Rose essential oil offers a soothing effect for the stressed and overburdened Aries. Individuals born under the Aries constellation are energetic and often at risk for stress and mental overload. The delicate fragrance of rose oil works by uplifting the mood to ease worry and prevent emotional and physical burnout.
- **Peppermint essential oil:** The Aries creative mind is constantly full of ideas. This constant flow of mental energy can sometimes result in lack of focus on one idea. This is where peppermint essential oil comes in because it can help remedy the situation. Diffusing peppermint oil into your space when having difficulty concentrating on a project or when experiencing mental blockage of ideas provides a burst of energy and renewed focus and helps keep the Aries mind on task. This need to gather scattered thoughts and ideas using peppermint essential oil may be necessary when embarking on a new project.
- **Geranium essential oil:** By nature, Aries individuals inadvertently have a tendency to become competitive with team members when working in a group. Geranium essential oil functions to re-focus their energies during group projects or tasks and therefore eliminate unnecessary competition and stress. This ultimately helps reduce the mental stress associated with a competitive mindset while also

restoring emotional equilibrium to the Aries team member.

- **Patchouli essential oil**: Patchouli oil is a great grounding medium. It is useful for clearing any negative feelings or mood and increasing cognition. It helps the Aries to remain grounded and focused rather than be subject to their passions and emotions.

- **Frankincense essential oil:** Frankincense oil is a strong aromatic oil that has dual functions as soothing and elevating. It promotes a peaceful and relaxing state of mind for the Aries by helping to quell their high energy drive and fiery nature when these two attributes are not needed.

Sample recipe for a positive and joyful essential oil blend for Aries:

"Joy and Positivity Spritz"

This sweet and floral blend of rose, geranium, and sweet orange essential oils combine to create a soothing fragrance that calms and uplifts the Aries' spirit to retain a positive and joyful outlook.

Ingredients

- 15 ml (half-ounce) Amber Spritz Bottle
- 10 ml of Fractionated Coconut Oil
- 2 drops of Rose Essential Oil
- 2 drops of Geranium Essential Oil
- 2 drops of Sweet Orange Essential Oil

Instructions

- Remove the spray cap from the half-ounce Amber Spritz Bottle.
- Add the specified drops of essential oils into the spritz bottle.
- Add the 10ml of fractionated coconut oil into the spritz bottle.
- Replace the spray cap on the spritz bottle and shake gently to mix thoroughly.
- The *Joy and Positivity Spritz* blend is now ready to be applied to the wrists and other pulse points to repel negative emotions, pessimism, and aggression.

[This blend may also be prepared as a roll-on by replacing the Amber Spritz Bottle with an Amber Glass Roll-on Bottle].

5.4 Birthstone and Crystals in Zodiac Self-Care

The role of crystals in zodiac astrology self-care is becoming more recognized and appreciated as we better understand their nature and power. Crystals are naturally formed elements within the earth's crust and are classified based on their structure, mineral composition, and specific properties. The process of formation of crystals (crystallization) may take millions of years. During the process, they are believed to absorb and store energy from the sun and other natural sources, which is capable of being transmitted, thus making them valuable tools in astrology and other spiritual practices. According to Judy Hall (2004), crystals possess celestial energy because they have been irradiated by the sun for millions of years. Therefore, there is a natural affinity and exchange of energy between crystals and the Sun. Every crystal is believed to have a distinct vibrational pattern that influences energy fields, emotions, and mental states. This vibrational energy property is the reason for the use of crystals in astrology. The concept of crystal astrology proposes that crystals are linked to zodiac signs based on their cosmic energies, thus offering personalized ways to align individuals from different zodiac signs with their optimal cosmic energies. Self-care and healing are two of the most prominent applications of crystal astrology.

Crystals for self-care

For self-care, each zodiac sign is associated with specific crystals that enhance positive traits and mitigate challenging attributes. For instance, Aries may benefit from red jasper for grounding and courage and howlite for calmness and peace, while Cancer might find comfort and emotional balance with moonstone. Furthermore, the Libra individual can use rose quartz to achieve harmony in relationships, and the Capricornian may seek focus and determination using garnet. In sum, by using crystals aligned with their astrological sign, individuals can elevate and enhance their personal strengths. This helps them maintain a sense of balance and general well-being while minimizing their weaknesses.

Crystals for healing

Crystals work together with the chakra system for healing. The healing power of crystals is often attributed to their ability to interact with the body's energy fields or chakras. This interaction helps to restore balance and harmony and eliminate illness. Crystals absorb, direct, and focus vibrational energy, making them helpful in reducing stress, enhancing meditation, and encouraging emotional healing. Specific crystals can aid in physical, emotional, and spiritual health by helping to balance energies. When the body's energies are balanced, illness is eliminated. Although scientific evidence on their effects is limited, crystals remain a popular tool for holistic healing and spiritual self-care. Holistic health practitioners can often help with finding suitable crystals to meet your needs.

As stated earlier, crystals possess energy absorbed from the sun and retained within the crystals for millions of years during its formation. The most practical and efficacious way to mobilize the power within the crystal is to hold or wear it (Hall, 2004). Holding or wearing the crystal next to the skin passes the crystal's vibrational energy into the wearer's subtle energy field and physical body. Crystals must be cleansed and charged to perform at their best. Most reputable crystal shops provide a crystal care guide for each purchase.

Crystals for the Zodiac Signs

Each zodiac constellation has several crystals associated with it. Conventionally, crystals were linked to distinct signs because of the similarity in energy resonance between the crystal and the zodiac sign or between the crystal and the month in which the sign fell, or because the crystal is aligned with the planet that ruled the sign or the month in which the sign fell. For example, the planet Mars (represented by the color red) rules the zodiac sign Aries. Therefore, red is the lucky color for Aries, and both Aries and Mars are aligned with the same gemstone, Ruby.

The various crystals associated with each zodiac sign are linked to different aspects of the sign. For instance, for each zodiac sign, there are different crystals for the Sun Sign (birthstone or sun crystal), the Moon Sign (lunar crystal), the Ascendant crystal (Crystal Mask), the abundance stone, and other companion crystals. Therefore, it is not uncommon to have five or more different crystals associated with a zodiac sign. For this book however, we will limit our discussion to the four most important categories of crystals for each sign, that is, the birthstone, abundance stone, ritual crystal, and companion crystal for positive traits and challenging traits.

Table 5A: Birthstones by month: Traditional vs Modern vs Mystical vs Ayurvedic

MONTH	TRADITIONAL	MODERN	MYSTICAL	AYUVEDIC
January	Garnet	Garnet	Emerald	Garnet
February	Amethyst	Amethyst	Bloodstone	Amethyst
March	Bloodstone	Aquamarine	Jade	Bloodstone
April	Diamond	Diamond	Opal	Diamond
May	Emerald	Emerald	Sapphire	Agate
June	Pearl	Alexandrite	Moonstone	Pearl
July	Ruby	Ruby	Ruby	Ruby
August	Banded Agate	Peridot	Diamond	Sapphire
September	Sapphire	Sapphire	Agate	Moonstone
October	Tourmaline	Opal	Jasper	Opal
November	Citrine	Yellow Topaz	Pearl	Topaz
December	Turquoise	Tanzanite	Zircon	Black Onyx

Classification of Crystals

For purposes of distinction in this book, the crystals discussed are classified loosely as precious gemstones (such as ruby, sapphire, and diamond), semi-precious gemstones (such as garnet, topaz, and peridot), and opaque stones/crystals (such as onyx, chalcedony, labradorite, and Lapis Lazuli).

Birthstones vs. Gemstones vs. Crystals

Birthstones are typically the prominent precious or semi-precious stone(s) that are aligned with a zodiac sign or the birth month for a zodiac sign. Table 5A depicts the traditional, modern, mystical, and ayurvedic crystals assigned to each month of the year and, by implication, each related zodiac sign.

Precious or rare stones are called gemstones. For example, ruby and diamond are two precious stones (gemstones), also the traditionally recognized birthstones of the zodiac sign Aries. Similarly, garnet, the birthstone for Capricorn, is a semi-precious stone.

Although they are both formed naturally in the earth and often used interchangeably, gemstones and crystals differ in structure, color, clarity, durability, classification, and value. For example, crystals have an ordered structure of repeating lattice patterns that form a geometric shape, whereas gemstones come in various shapes and sizes. Also, a gemstone is valued by its rarity, beauty, durability, and cut and thus tends to be more expensive than a crystal, which is typically uncut and less rare. Table 5 below summarizes the main differences between crystals and gemstones. The principal point to remember is that most gemstones are crystals, but not all crystals are gemstones. For example, sand, sugar, and salt crystals are not considered gemstones at all. Table 5A is a summarized comparison table highlighting the differences between gemstones and crystals.

Table 5B: Comparison of gemstones vs crystals

Attribute	Gemstone	Crystal
Structure	Can exist as crystalline (defined structure) or as amorphous (no defined structure)	An ordered, repeating, lattice pattern of atoms that form a geometric shape.
Shape	Disordered arrangement of atoms with so specific shape	Geometrical arrangement of atoms
Classification	Classified by their physical and chemical properties, including mineral composition, rarity, and value.	Classified by their shape and structural arrangement
Color	Muted colors	Vibrant colors
Clarity	Less clear and less brilliant	Clearer (more transparent) and more brilliant due to more light reflection ability
Durability	Less durable (due to weaker covalent bonds)	More durable (lasts longer due to stronger ionic bonds between atoms and lattices)
Abundance/Rarity	Typically, less common/available in nature (rarer)	Typically, more common in nature (less rare)
Value	Can be very valuable and expensive, depending on its rarity, cut, beauty, and durability)	Typically, less valuable
Uses	Often cut and polished for use as jewelry or as ornamental or decorative items. Example diamond necklace	Often used in industrial and technological applications due to their strength, durability, and purity. Example, quartz crystals are used for computer parts and timekeeping devices due to their precise structure and constant (reliable) vibrations.

Tips for purchasing and using your zodiac crystals

- Uncut stones and crystals are best purchased at a crystal shop, whereas rarer crystals (precious and semi-precious gemstones) are best purchased from a gem store, jewelry store, or a trusted internet source.
- Handling crystals is the best way to get a "feel" of which one is attracted to your energy (that is, the one whose vibrations complement your subtle energy field).
- Wearing your zodiac crystal/gemstone is the best way to harness and release its energy and power.
- Every crystal must be cleansed from negative vibes before and after each use and re-energized (re-dedicated) after each use.
- Ways to cleanse and re-energize/re-dedicate crystals (Hall, 2004):
  - For crystals that are impervious to water or moisture, hold the crystals under running water for a few minutes to cleanse them, then place them on a clean surface in the sun to re-energize them.
  - For crystals that may be damaged by water (such as porous or friable crystals), place them in a bowl of dry rice or on a carnelian for a few hours to cleanse them, then remove them and place them on a clean surface in the sun's rays to re-energize them.
  - Once the crystal has been cleansed and re-energized using any of the two methods above, re-dedicate it by holding it in your hands for a few

minutes and using positive intentions from within you to dedicate it to the highest good that comes to mind (For example, while holding the crystal in your hand, picture it infused with and surrounded by pure white light, and clearly state your intention for the crystal audibly. This process will re-dedicate/reprogram the crystal).

- Wearing your crystal next to your skin consistently and cleansing it regularly would help you reap the maximum benefits from its energy (power).

- To attract wealth and good fortune, wear or carry your ***abundance crystal*** on your body next to your skin consistently, or place it in the **FAR-LEFT** corner of your room.

- To ensure the release of the most power from your sunstone (birthstone) or simply from your favorite crystal, place it under your pillow while sleeping at night and hold it or wear it during meditation.

- For healing benefits, you should place the relevant crystal over the affected part of your body needing healing for 15-20 minutes daily.

- You must cleanse your crystal before using it for yourself if other people handle your crystal or if you use your crystal to heal other people. This cleansing ritual is necessary to remove any lingering energies from the other person or persons.

- Most precious gemstones have a semi-precious clear or opaque substitute. Here are some examples.

Table 5C: Gemstone substitutes

Gemstone	Substitute (semi-precious gem or crystal)
Ruby	Garnet
Diamond	Clear Quartz
Sapphire	Lapis lazuli
Emerald	Peridot

Aries' Ascendant Crystals

The Ascendant in zodiac astrology is described as the zodiac sign rising over the eastern horizon at the moment of a person's birth. The zodiac sign for each ascendant is believed to be ruled by a planet or ancient god/goddess who bestowed a specific blessing or virtue on the person.

The Ascendant sign represents the face that one presents to the outside world. You may visualize it as a "personality mask" worn to cover/hide their true personality. The Ascendant personality could be very different from the true nature bestowed on them by their Sun sign. In other words, the Sun sign represents a person's "true personality" or "ego," whereas the Ascendant sign represents their "masked personality" or "alter ego." When a person's Sun sign does not fit the way other people perceive them, it indicates that they may be unconsciously reflecting their Ascendant sign. For example, an Aries with a Pisces Ascendant may be perceived as carefree, emotional, and sympathetic to the outside world when, in reality, they are focused, assertive, and insensitive to others' feelings. When Aries is the Ascendant sign of someone whose Sun sign is from any of the other zodiac signs, they usually would hide behind a bold, brash, assertive, and rumbunctious personality, which they present to the world to mask the true nature of their Sun sign.

Like the Sun sign, each Ascendant sign is associated with its own crystal(s). The Ascendant crystal is a powerful tool for self-development and personal empowerment. Tapping into the Ascendant crystal can enhance the benefits associated with their Ascendant sign. Below are some specific crystals associated with the Aries Ascendant.

- **Jasper crystal**: works well in tempering the bold, domineering, rumbunctious, and impatient Aries Ascendant by helping them maintain a sense of proportion and calm.
- **Jasper + solar crystal + lunar crystal**: This combination of crystals would soften the egotistical Aries Ascendant.
- **Mookaite Jasper crystal**: This crystal can enhance the inborn moon-inspired qualities of courage, initiative, and assertiveness associated with the Aries Ascendant.

5.5 The Chakras

Now, let us discuss a crucial concept central to meditation and various zodiac self-care techniques – the chakras.

The Concept of Chakras

The concept of chakras is based on the principle that the human body is not just a physical entity but also comprises an outer layer of subtle energy described as a surrounding pulsating electromagnetic energy force field that appears as a rainbow-like shield around each person. This encapsulating "subtle energy" field which is only visible to the naked eye with special spiritual training, is also referred to as an "aura" and gives the human body the appearance of being luminous when visualized. The surrounding energy field (aura) described above interacts with the physical body by flowing through seven regions of concentrated spiraling energy centers known as "chakras." Therefore, chakras may be defined as the energy centers of the body through which the aural electromagnetic energy field flows to interact with the physical body (Mercier, 2007). In other words, chakras are concentrated energy centers that act as both reservoirs and channels for electromagnetic energy to flow between the aura and the physical body. The concept of the chakra has its origins in Hinduism and Buddhism.

The word "chakra" is derived from a Sanskrit word meaning "wheels of light," which is actually how the energy force field surrounding the human body appears. [Sanskrit: An ancient Indian language used since 1200BC, in which the Hindu scriptures and ancient Indian poems are written, and from which many Indian languages are derived]. There are seven (7) main chakras of the human body and they interact with seven (7) ductless endocrine glands and the lymphatic system by instilling (channeling in) good energy (positive energy) and expelling (removing/channeling out) unwanted energy (negative energy).

Chakra definition and roles

Chakras are specific points in the body where vital energy flows and intersects. They are commonly defined as "the energy centers in the body". Chakras are similar to energy repository stations through which the body transmits and receives physical, emotional, and spiritual energy. These chakra energy centers are responsible for different aspects of our physical, emotional, and spiritual well-being. Each chakra is associated with a particular area of the body and a color of the spectrum.

Types of Chakras

The nature and classification of the chakras are tied to Indian Yogic teachings. There are seven (7) major chakras, multiple minor chakras, and one important chakra called the Alta Major.

The major chakras are associated with the seven main endocrine glands of the human body and are perceived to be the "initiators" of crucial body functions because they are closely involved in maintaining the body's biochemical balance.

The minor chakras interact with and control vital bodily functions. They are perceived as the energy "defenders" of the human body because they absorb and release subtle energy to keep the body healthy.

The Alta Major is located at the base of the back of the head (skull), that is, at the nape of the neck. It is defined as the energy point for memory, including distant memory, past-life recall memories, and race and survival memory inherited from our ancestors.

The combination of the major chakras, minor chakras, Alta Major, auric field, and interconnecting energy lines running between the physical body and the surrounding energy fields make up the "matrix" of all human life.

Role & Importance of the Chakras

- The most crucial role of each chakra is that of balancing various aspects of the subtle life-force energies within an individual's aura and transforming this energy into a form that is acceptable to the individual's body because it is in a harmonious or resonant state with the other chakras.
- Each chakra transmits energy communications (messages) between the aura and the surrounding environment. Therefore, every individual is connected to their environment through the subtle electromagnetic impulses channeled between their aura, their chakras, and the environment.

The functional states of the chakras

The chakras can exist and operate in either of four functional states:

- **Active state**: The active chakra functions optimally and displays a healthy inflow and outflow of energy. A person with an active chakra is typically fit and healthy because all the areas controlled by that chakra are in harmony with the other chakras. This individual will also have a vibrant energy field.

- **Underactive state**: The underactive chakra performs sub-optimally and, therefore, needs stimulation to achieve the active state. The affected individual is noted to be in an unhealthy state in their physical body or auric energy field, usually due to a lack or insufficiency of some physical factor or subtle bio-energy.
- **Passive/balanced state**: The chakra in a passive or balanced state is either at rest or exists in a harmonious balance of energy input and output. In either case, this chakra is balanced (healthy) but not activated.
- **Overactive state**: The overactive chakra is overstimulated. Overstimulation usually results from prolonged attempts to remove imbalances (negative energies) from the physical body that are detrimental to the overall well-being of the affected individual. It is expected to diagnose overactive chakras in chronic illness or addiction.

Chakras and Self-Care

The concept of chakra in self-care derives from the premise that in order to maintain our general health and well-being and prevent illness/disease, the seven chakras must be nourished correctly. The chakra system is important for understanding all forms of holistic healing including the use of crystals (crystal healing), herbs and oils (aromatherapy), color, sound, reiki, hands-on healing, acupuncture, shiatsu, tai chi, and other effective self-heal methods used within the complementary and alternative medicine (CAM) practice. In traditional Chinese medicine, similar energy-based healing concepts to the chakra concept include acupuncture, the Yin and Yang Theory, and the Five Element Theory (Mercier, 2007). Chakra healing is mainly associated with Indian Yogic teachings.

The Seven Main Chakras & and Their Crystal Associations

As stated above, each chakra is associated with a particular body area/location and a specific spectrum color. Among other uses, crystals and stones (gemstones) are used to clear stagnant energies, revitalize pure and positive energies, balance the chakras, and heal the body. Crystals and stones can help balance the chakras by interacting with the body's energy fields and channeling them in a manner that promotes harmony and balance. When used as chakra-balancing tools, crystals, and stones help to open the chakras. As a rule, the selection of crystals or stones corresponds with the chakra's associated color.

Although some minor chakras have been identified, there are seven (7) major chakras. Below is a list of the seven (7) primary chakras of the human body and their associated balancing crystals/stones and colors.

1. The Base/Root Chakra (Muladhara)

Crystal/Stone: Red Jasper; Black Tourmaline; Smoky Quartz; Hematite
Purpose: Grounding; Self-identity; Financial independence; Financial Safety
Chakra Color: **Red**
Associated Essential Oils: Cedarwood; Patchouli; Myrrh
Associated Yoga Poses: Warrior; Triangle; Eagle

2. The Sacral Chakra (Svadisthana)

Crystal/Stone: Carnelian; Citrine; Amber; Tiger's Eye; Garnet
Purpose: Sexuality; Creativity; Abundance; Enthusiasm
Chakra Color: **Orange**
Associated Essential Oils: Sandalwood; Jasmine; Rose oil
Associated Yoga Poses: Twisting triangle; Extended lateral angle; Pose of Shiva

3. The Solar Plexus Chakra (Manipura)

Crystal/Stone: Tiger's Eye; Citrine; Yellow Aventurine; Topaz
Purpose: Self-confidence; Self-esteem; Personality development
Chakra Color: **Yellow/Golden**
Associated Essential Oils: Clary sage; Juniper; Geranium
Associated Yoga Poses: Cow pose; Sitting spinal twist; Camel pose

4. The Heart Chakra (Anahata):

Crystal/Stone: Green Aventurine; Rose Quartz; Rhodonite
Purpose: Love; Joy; Compassion; Inner Fulfillment; Inner Peace
Chakra Color: Green
Associated Essential Oils: Rose, Melissa; Neroli
Associated Yoga Poses: Cobra/Raised cobra pose; head-to-knee forward bend; Fish pose

5. The Throat Chakra (Vishuddha):

Crystal/Stone: Blue Lace Agate; Aquamarine; Lapis Lazuli; Blue Sodalite
Purpose: Communication; Self-Expression
Chakra Color: Turquoise
Associated Essential Oils: Lavender; Chamomile; Rosemary/Thyme/Sage
Associated Yoga Poses: Bow pose; Lion pose; Sitting forward bend pose

6. The Third Eye (Brow) Chakra (Ajna):

Crystal/Stone: Labradorite; Lapis Lazuli; Sodalite
Purpose: Intuition; Clairvoyance; Extra-Sensory Perception; Wisdom
Chakra Color: Deep Blue (Indigo)
Associated Essential Oils: Passion flower; Papaya; Tarragon; Frankincense; Basil
Associated Yoga Poses: Dog, face-down pose; Yoga mudra in the Lotus position; Plough pose

7. The Crown Chakra (Sahasrara):

Crystal/Stone: Amethyst; Clear Quartz; Moonstone
Purpose: Intelligence; Self-Awareness; Divine Consciousness; Spiritual enlightenment
Chakra Color: Violet (Purple); White
Associated Essential Oils: Ylang-ylang; Rosewood; Linden/Lime blossom; Lotus/Water lily
Associated Yoga Poses: Headstand; Crane pose; Shoulder stand

Note: To utilize crystals for chakra-balancing, place them on or near the corresponding chakra location while meditating or carry them with you throughout the day, preferably in contact with or close to the skin.

Table 5D: The major chakras and their associations

Chakra	Influencing color	Element association	Sensory association	Endocrine gland association
Crown Chakra (Sahasrara)	**Violet** (or Gold)	Spirit	All the senses	Pineal gland
Brow Chakra (Third Eye) (Ajna)	**Deep Blue**	Spirit	Extra-Sensory Perception (ESP)	Pituitary gland
Throat Chakra (Vishuddha)	**Turquoise**	Ether (Akasha)	Hearing	Thyroid & Parathyroid glands
Heart Chakra (Anahata)	**Green** (or Pink)	Air	Touch	Thymus
Solar Plexus Chakra (Manipura)	**Yellow**	Fire	Sight	Pancreas
Sacral Chakra (Svadisthana)	**Orange**	Water	Taste	Adrenal glands
Base Chakra (Muladhara)	**Red**	Earth	Smell	Testes/Ovaries

The Dominant Chakra for Each Zodiac sign

All 12 zodiac signs draw strength from the seven major chakras in the body. Still, only one chakra dominates each zodiac sign. Below is a summary of the dominant chakra for each zodiac sign.

- **Aries**: Solar plexus chakra. The solar plexus is the dominant chakra location for Aries. The solar plexus chakra is located in the upper abdomen. It is believed to be the source of self-confidence (self-belief), self-esteem (self-worth), personality development, and power. Self-confidence, Self-esteem, Personality development. The color associated with the solar plexus chakra is yellow.

- **Taurus**: Heart chakra. Members of the Taurus zodiac sign have strong green heart chakras, which are associated with the color green. The heart chakra's energy gives them strong empathy skills and helps them build good bonds.
- **Gemini**: Throat chakra. The throat chakra regulates communication and creativity and is the controlling chakra in Gemini individuals. As a result of its influence, Geminis are great orators. They can express themselves easily. Their communication skills and great verbal networking ability help Gemini to effortlessly gain other people's trust. The color associated with the throat chakra is turquoise blue.
- **Cancer**: Third eye chakra. Cancer is heavily influenced by the sixth chakra (also known as the "third eye chakra" or "brow chakra"), which is considered to be the gateway to the center of the soul. The third eye chakra, located on the forehead, endows Cancerians with the spiritual ability to see visions. The color linked to the third eye (brow) chakra is deep blue.
- **Leo**: Crown chakra. Leos have the innate gift of a strong crown chakra. Their spiritually heightened crown chakras help Leo individuals to think, understand, and process information rapidly, thus their ability to solve problems and implement solutions quickly. The color associated with the crown chakra is violet.

- **Virgo**: Throat chakra. Similar to Geminis, Virgos possess dominant throat chakras and are blessed with remarkable public speaking and communication skills as well. The throat chakra color is turquoise blue.
- **Libra**: Heart chakra. The Libra's most powerful chakra center is the heart chakra. A strong heart chakra favors emotional healing and well-being, which in turn fosters the formation of healthy emotional bonds with others. The heart chakra is linked with the color green.
- **Scorpio**: Solar plexus chakra. Like Aries, the Scorpio's dominant chakra center is the solar plexus chakra. The tough solar plexus chakra gives Scorpios immense control over their emotions, which assists them in battling and overcoming their tendency to be fearful. The solar plexus chakra is linked to yellow color.
- **Sagittarius**: Sacral chakra. Sagittarians have a potent sacral chakra. The sacral chakra is located in the lower abdomen, approximately three inches below the navel, and placed retro-peritoneally (in the back) in the lumbar spine region. This chakra center is under the control of the planet Jupiter. Jupiter is linked to expansion (growth), abundance (luck), and knowledge (wisdom). As a result of Jupiter's "good fortune," Sagittarians are usually very optimistic and passionate individuals. The sacral chakra is associated with orange color.
- **Capricorn**: Root/Base chakra. Capricornians have the most robust root (base) chakra centers. The base chakra is located at the base of the spine, deep within

the pelvic floor, in the perineum between the anus and the genitals. The ruling planet for Capricorn is Saturn, which is strongly linked to the Earth element and also known for discipline, structure, and responsibility. The combined influence of Planet Saturn and the Capricornian's firm root (base) chakra endows Capricornians with formidable mental and physical well-being as well as the following characteristics: practical, down-to-earth, and unpretentious (candid). The color associated with the root chakra is red.

- **Aquarius**: Root/Base chakra. The root chakra (represented by the red color) is also the presiding chakra center in Aquarians. This provides them support and gives them the ability to remain grounded, reliable, and sturdy.
- **Pisces**: Sacral chakra. Both Sagittarians and Pisceans have vigorous sacral chakras, but the sacral chakra has a much stronger influence on Pisces compared to Sagittarius. Specifically, the sacral chakra has the most effect on the Pisces' sex life and sensuality. This is why Pisceans are well known for their high sex drive, intuitive powers, and creativity compared to all the other zodiac signs. The sacral chakra color is orange.

How to Gain Chakra Awareness & Diagnose Chakra Imbalances

Understanding your chakras (chakra awareness) involves exploring the condition, performance, and health of your chakras. One who has chakra awareness is perfectly tuned into their chakras. This can be an effective way to tap into your mind, body, and spirit. (Mercier, 2007). To understand your chakra state, you should monitor which chakras react significantly when experiencing a stressful situation. You can also observe and note which chakra is constantly activated when you have a chronic illness or recurring problems.

Below are some examples of symptoms that may help diagnose unbalanced chakras.

1. Crown Chakra

- Weak crown chakra: Impaired ability to think rationally and clearly under stress.
- Unbalanced crown chakra: Impatience and impaired discernment in spiritual matters, for example, seeking the benefits of spiritual growth without first nurturing your spiritual health

2. Brow Chakra

- Underactive brow chakra: Lack of vision and organization in your life; Impaired ability to establish focus and direction in many areas of your life.
- Overactive brow chakra: You are prone to having constant nightmares.

3. Throat Chakra

- Weak throat chakra: You have impaired speech or

you stutter; You have difficulty being truthful; You do not easily express your feelings and emotions.

- Overactive throat chakra: You speak hastily without thinking; Your words are often harsh and hurtful even when you do not really mean them.

4. Heart Chakra

- Weak heart chakra: You have a slow heart rate; You sometimes feel that your heart has skipped a beat (Note that these are signs of both a weak heart chakra and a weak physical heart – that is, physical heart problems)
- Overactive heart chakra: You often have a fast heart rate; Your pulse races in stressful situations; You are often ruddy-faced (reddened face).

5. Solar Plexus Chakra

- Inactive solar plexus chakra: You often feel incapable and helpless under pressure; You have a queasy feeling or "butterflies" in your stomach when under pressure; You feel dread when under pressure.
- Overactive solar plexus chakra: You crave to be in control (control freak); You are often domineering and intimidating.

6. Sacral Chakra

- Underactive sacral chakra: You lack personal joy in

your life; You have a gloomy perspective to life; You
are often depressed.

- Hyperactive sacral chakra: You get frustrated easily;
  You are often tense.

7. Base Chakra

- Weak/Underactive base chakra: You perceive
  yourself as having a lack of self-control; You
  experience body dysmorphia; You criticize your body
  shape, size, or weight; You feel inadequate physically
  due to your perceived lack of self-control.
- Overactive base chakra: You have an explosive
  temper; You get angry at the slightest provocation;
  You are not in control of your mood and temper (you
  are easily overwhelmed by your emotions).

These are just some examples to guide your understanding of
your chakra. I recommend working with an experienced
chakra expert or healer to gain a more personalized awareness
of the health of your chakras.

Simple chakra-balancing exercise

Disclaimer: This exercise is a simple wellness exercise similar
to a yoga stretch or pose. It cannot be performed on oneself.
You need someone else (preferably an experienced yoga or
chakra expert) to perform it on you. This exercise does not
claim to heal any illnesses or mitigate any symptoms. It is not
an alternative treatment for any disease condition. You should
always consult your healthcare provider for any symptoms or
health conditions.

1. The client assumes a comfortable position on a hard chair or stool.
2. The chakra expert stands behind the seated client.
3. The expert places his/her right hand just under the occipital bone at the base of the skull's rear (back).
4. Simultaneously, the expert supports the client's forehead with the left hand.
5. The expert then uses the right hand to gently stretch the back of the client's neck by giving a little tug with the right hand at the base of the skull while gently supporting the forehead with the left hand, all in one simultaneous motion.

Result: The above chakra balancing stretch brings all seven main chakras into one central, vertical alignment.

5.6 Affirmations and Mantras (Chants)

Affirmations are short, simple, positive, self-empowering, and confidence-boosting phrases or statements that people repeat to themselves to help create an optimistic mindset by moving thoughts and actions in a positive direction. They are short phrases that can be repeated over and over throughout the day to change how one thinks and feels about themselves (Goldman, 2022). They can be said aloud, written down, or silently reflected upon. In a 2016 research study, Cascio et al. proposed that self-affirmation works by stimulating the brain regions that are associated with processing reward, and its effect is further strengthened by future orientation. Affirmations derive from psychology and are often used in tandem with mindfulness. They are easy to practice anywhere and at any time, so they are readily accessible for coping with stressful situations throughout the day (Moore, 2019). Positive affirmations are used to challenge negative or unhelpful thoughts and have been identified as valuable tools for managing depression symptoms. By consistently repeating positive phrases and statements, people reinforce positive thinking by redirecting negative thought patterns. Evidence-based benefits of using positive affirmations include stress reduction, increased self-esteem, and maintaining calm and balance. Examples of daily affirmations include, "I am complete and content," "I am worthy of love and happiness," "I am capable of achieving my goals," and "I choose to focus on the present moment and feel at peace." One of the most effective ways of using positive affirmations is to look at yourself in the mirror while repeating affirmative words loudly to yourself.

Mantras are words, sounds, or invocations in any language that assist the individual in focusing concentration and deepening meditation while uniting him or her with a higher power. Mercier (2007) defines mantras as "poetic hymns, incantations, or prayers that are repeated many times, either silently or loudly." They originated from Eastern religious practices and have been used for many years. Mantras are associated with mysticism and spirituality and aim to release the mind from thoughts to facilitate inner peace. They may or may not have a translatable meaning to the user. Examples of mantras include single words such as "Om," "Eck," "Shalom," (or "peace"), "Eli", "Elohim," "Alleluia, "Amen," or Sanskrit phrases such as "Om Namah Shivaya" which can be interpreted as bowing to our true highest selves.

Although positive affirmations and mantras are used interchangeably, they are vastly different in terms of their origins and applications. Positive affirmations originated in the 1970s when neuroscientists sought to combine psychotherapy with everyday language to devise a means of consciously re-wiring thought patterns towards the more desired goals of positivity, optimism, and confidence (Institute for Integrative Nutrition, 2024). They are meaningful words or phrases to motivate the person reciting them. Mantras, on the other hand, originate from Eastern meditative practices, as seen in Buddhism and Hinduism. Mantras may be sounds or words and typically do not have any literal, translatable meaning. Despite their differences, positive affirmations and personal mantras, when effective, achieve similar objectives, including the following:

- Increase positive thoughts and emotions
- Boost self-confidence
- Improve interpersonal relationships
- Enhance mental clarity
- Improve problem-solving skills
- Increase the likelihood of personal success
- Reduce stress and anxiety

Practice: How to perform a simple meditative mantra (chant)

- Locate a quiet space that is free from visual and audio distractions.
- Assume a comfortable seated and poised position (most people prefer to sit or stand according to their religious practices)

- Using focused (targeted) breathing, achieve a relaxed state.
- Breathe rhythmically and quietly through your nostrils and completely into your abdomen (complete yoga breathing, similar to diaphragmatic breathing).
- Begin to hum a soft and gentle mantra of your choosing, for example, "Om"
- Imagine that you are engaging your throat chakra as you hum
- Continue to maintain a relaxed and passive mindset toward any distracting thoughts or visions as you hum

Great job! You have just completed a meditative mantra exercise. Have you noticed that it is nearly impossible to do any meditation exercise without employing breathwork exercises? There is much more intriguing information about the chakras and how they can be harnessed to optimize every aspect of one's life. However, for this book, the discussion will be restricted to the best use of the chakras to live your best life as an Aries. If you would like to delve deeper into understanding the chakra system and zodiac astrology, be sure to **follow this author's profile on your favorite bookstore** and **sign up for the fan newsletter** so that you will be among the first fans to be notified and given a free preview of her anticipated upcoming comprehensive astrology book about the use of chakra balancing and crystals to get the best out of each zodiac sign.

5.7 Aries: How to Use Your Self-Care Tools

In this segment, we will discuss specifically how Aries members can maximize the use of all the self-care tools we have discussed thus far. Remember that while self-care is a continuous process from the beginning to the end of the day, one must set aside a specific period each day for meditation, self-reflection, or journaling.

- **Always Begin with Relaxation & Meditation**: Always begin with attaining total body relaxation using any combination of breathing exercises and mindfulness meditation. Being in a relaxed state of mind opens the mind to be receptive to energy exchange to balance the chakras.

- **Your Power Color**: **Red**. Colors are reservoirs of energy derived from the sun's rays. Therefore, it makes sense that the energy harnessed from the colors we surround ourselves with can affect our subtle bio-energies and chakra balance. Red is the color of the planet Mars (also known as "The Red Planet"), which oversees the Aries zodiac sign. Red is exciting, passionate, and energetic. It is an unforgettable color, demanding attention and eliciting a sense of adventure and an eagerness for life. This explains the natural characteristics that Aries individuals are known for: bold, strong, outspoken, assertive, enthusiastic, determined, tenacious, adventurous, creative, and pioneering.

Red serves as a positive reinforcement for Aries. It amplifies their natural attributes discussed above. The more you surround yourself with shades of red as an Aries, the more intense your natural powers and attributes will be. So, infuse touches of red into your space as much as you can. A touch of red in your fashion would go a long way in empowering you for the day – a colorful top with splashes of cherry red, a coral necklace, a pair of maroon heels, a dash of blood red lipstick, a ruby bracelet, a burgundy scarf, or scarlet scrunches for your hair, etc. Surrounded by your power color and fortified by a piece of your power crystal in your pocket, nothing can hold you back from conquering every challenge in your path throughout the day!

- **Your Birthstones/Gemstones**: **Ruby** and **Diamond**. The Aries sun sign is aligned with two gemstones (birthstones) – Ruby and Diamond. The passionate and vigorous Aries nature is reflected in the fiery red Ruby, also the signature gem for the Aries ruling planet Mars.

Ruby

Diamond

The Ruby effect: Ruby has a stimulating effect on Aries and resonates with their innate passion and drive. Because it aligns with Aries's personality, ideals, and purpose in life, Ruby reinforces their fearlessness, strength, focus, and dynamic leadership potential. It also fuels their sense of adventure and curiosity, often resulting in remarkable creativity and pioneer work in their field of expertise. On the downside, the Ruby effect may not always be advantageous for Aries. If unbalanced or unchecked, it may result in over-stimulation of Aries's personality, resulting in stress and a propensity for anger with minimal provocation and increased self-centeredness.

Diamond effect: The diamond birthstone offsets (counteracts) the Ruby effect by introducing a calmness that enhances thoughtfulness and consideration for others. This balances out the selfishness that Ruby's overstimulation may trigger. When using this gemstone correctly and consistently, you will sense a softening in your approach to situations and dealings with others. The Diamond effect also augments communication skills, which promotes bonding in Aries's relationships (Hall, 2004). It is also associated with clarity of mind, strength, and invincibility. In summary, diamonds are synonymous with strength, clarity, and invincibility for Aries.

- **Your Healing Crystals**: **Amethyst**, **Clear Quartz**, **Luminescent Fire Agate**, and **Fire Agate**. These are healing crystals whose energies potentiate the Aries's subtle energy.

  - **Amethyst**: Aries is closely associated with the head and thus strongly influenced by the Crown Chakra. You are, therefore, prone to headaches, trigeminal neuralgia, and other similar ailments that affect the head and the face. This crystal is used to soothe headaches, a common ailment of Aries individuals. It can be placed on the forehead for about 15 to 20 minutes to soothe the headache and promote relaxation.

Amethyst

- **Clear Quartz**: It is used with other Aries-compatible crystals for ritual healing. For example, the combination of a piece of clear quartz crystal above the head, an amethyst over the forehead, a piece of kunzite over the heart, a citrine over the solar plexus, and a smoky quartz placed pointing down between the feet while lying down in a supine position is believed to eliminate stress, negativity, and insomnia, and usher in peace to your body and space.
- **Luminescent Fire Agate**: Luminescent fire agate is a powerful *grounding crystal* for Aries and is considered a proven all-around healing crystal. It may also be used for a protection ritual against ill luck.
- **Fire Agate**: This is an excellent *meditation crystal* for Aries because it has a calming and mellowing effect on the Aries's subtle energy rhythm. It is also believed to stabilize the endocrine system and prevent stress and exhaustion.

- **Your Abundance Stone: Carnelian**. The abundance stone for Aries is the Carnelian (Carnelian orange). Abundance stones, by description, attract good fortune and material blessings (wealth). Carnelian is a known powerful abundance stone associated with boosting confidence, increasing motivation and creativity, and manifesting abundance. For maximum benefit, use your carnelian in these two ways:

  - worn in contact with your skin or body (typically, it is set as polished, faceted gemstone into a ring, earring, necklace, or bracelet) or in the pocket of your clothing next to your skin.
  - Placed in the far-left corner of an entry room into your home.

Carnelian

Natural polished carnelian stone

In addition to being an abundance stove for Aries, the carnelian crystal is also known to enhance motivation and creativity.

- **Your Ritual Stone: Fire Agate**. Fire agate is the ritual stone for Aries. Ritual stones are potent stones that vibrate intensely and harmoniously with a person's bioenergy or with a specific zodiac sign or chakra. Therefore, they are used to amplify specific rituals such as blessing rituals, protection rituals, creativity rituals, good luck rituals, etc. For the Aries individual, fire agate enhances the balance between courage and contentment while also keeping them grounded and dedicated to their purpose or mission.

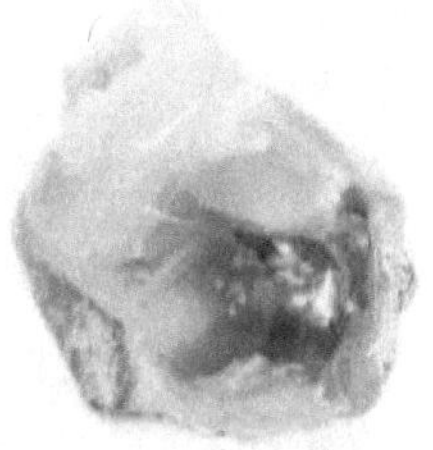

Fire Agate crystal stone

- **Your Companion & Substitute Crystals**:

Other companion crystals that work well with Aries for multiple purposes include the following:

- **Pink Tourmaline**: heart protector (encourages love; dissolves emotional pain); aphrodisiac
- **Aragonite**: mental flexibility and clarity
- **Aqua aura**: an iridescent crystal for spiritual enlightenment
- **Kunzite**: brings love and peace into relationships; humility; tolerance
- **Green Calcite**: anti-stress crystal for Aries
- **Red Jasper**: grounding crystal; enhances courage
- **Citrine** – boosts confidence; used for manifesting

abundance. Citrine complements the power of the Carnelian gemstone.

- **Bloodstone** – Promotes courage and helps with decision-making. May substitute for Ruby.
- **Jade** – Jade (also known as the green gemstone) is strongly connected to the heart chakra and allows it to nurture love, compassion, and self-love. This makes jade a powerful tool for personal growth and transformation. Jade helps to calm Aries's fiery temperament by offering balance and promoting inner peace, tranquility, and clarity. It also has the added benefit of being a powerful healing agent that balances bodily fluids, cleanses organs, and removes toxins.
- **Sapphire** – Sapphire is a gemstone that symbolizes wisdom and serenity. It calms the Aries' impulsive nature and helps promote self-discipline.

- **Your Essential Oils and Herbs**:

Aries may use various essential oils and herbs for different purposes. In this segment, we will discuss them.

Essential Oils:

Now, let us take a detailed look into the two signature essential oils for members of the Aries zodiac sign: Rosemary (signature warm essential oil) and Bergamot (signature calming/soothing essential oil), followed by examples of other Aries-compatible essential oils.

Rosemary (*Rosmarinus officinalis)*:

- Both soothing and uplifting effects; Good for reversing emotional burnout
- Eases stress (soothing effect) and uplifts mood (restorative effect) to prevent emotional burnout. (Ilana, 2021).

Bergamot oil (citrus bergamia):

- Extracted from fresh bergamot orange fruit
- It has a citrus scent with a fresh floral note similar to the smell of sweet orange peel oil or lemon/lime oil.
- Bergamot oil is used to relieve stress and anxiety, increase mental alertness, reduce joint pain and other inflammatory conditions, and facilitate wound healing (Healthline, 2018).
- It helps to balance out the Aries's tendency for impatience and irritation
- It may also be used for grounding (centering) the mind.

A popular way of using essential oils and herb extracts is by mixing a selection of oils into a blend. Essential oil blends tailored for Aries may include the two signature essential oils (rosemary, bergamot) plus a variety of Aries-compatible oils such as: black pepper, black spruce, fragonia, frankincense, lemon, and Roman chamomile. Others include rose oil, peppermint oil, geranium oil, patchouli, and frankincense oil. These blends may be prepared for use in diffusers, scented roll-ons, spritzes, air freshener sprays, etc. Most aromatherapy practitioners and reputable stores will advise customers on which combination of oils or herbs to blend (mix) that matches their personality.

Below is a brief description of the primary uses of popular essential oils for preparing blends for Aries individuals.

- **Rose oil**: Eases stress and uplifts mood to avoid emotional burnout for Aries. A dab of dilute rose oil at pulse points (neck, wrists, back of knees) works wonders with unwinding after a long day at work.
- **Peppermint oil**: For Aries individuals, peppermint oil provides an energy boost and helps to refocus energies and thoughts to enhance creativity. It also promotes mental clarity and focus.
- **Geranium oil**: Helps to re-focus energies, reduce stress, and restore emotional balance.
- **Patchouli oil**: It helps to clear negative feelings or moods and increases cognition. It is excellent for grounding and centering hyper-energetic zodiac signs like Aries.
- **Frankincense oil**: Frankincense oil serves a dual function of soothing and elevating. It promotes peace

and relaxation and provides balance to fire signs like Aries.

- **Cinnamon oil**: Cinnamon oil inspires warmth and passion, uplifting the Aries spirit.

Herbs:

There are many suitable herbs for Aries, and they include the following:

- **Lavender**: Soothing and calming. It helps soothe Aries' fiery energy. It also reduces stress and impatience. Usually brewed and ingested as tea.
- **Chamomile**: A grounding herb that brings peace and balance to Aries' intense energy. It is a popular grounding herb that is typically ingested as a tea.
- **Basil (herb)**: Stimulates mental agility and boosts focus.
- **Ginger**: Spicy Ginger is known to promote vitality and stimulate energy. It promotes digestion and may be used as a prophylactic for stomach troubles. It is often available as ginger tea or ginger-infused sweets and treats.
- **Cinnamon:** Cinnamon amplifies energy, vitality, and mental focus. It adds a warm, invigorating quality that aligns with Aries's passionate nature.
- **Thyme**: Thyme is thought to enhance courage and bravery.

- **Your Symbolic Animal**: The Ram

The Ram is the symbol of the Aries zodiac sign. As discussed in earlier chapters of this book, this animal embodies the sheer strength, determination, courage, and leadership that form the basis of Aries' assertive and leadership qualities. The ram's origin as Aries's symbol is discussed in chapter one, section 1.4.

- **Your Familial Animal**: The deer

The deer is Aries's familial (guide) animal. It symbolizes intuition, grace, and vigilance (awareness), balancing Aries's intense energy with sensitivity and awareness.

- **Your Talisman/Charm**: Ram symbol, Iron talisman, Arrow symbol

Most Aries's talismans and charms are made with some representation of the ram symbol. They are typically blessed or dedicated and worn close to the body as a chain, trinket, necklace, bracelet, ring, etc. The purpose is to amplify the energies and ruling powers associated with the Aries zodiac sign, often for good luck. Below are the best charm and talisman ideas for Aries:

- **Ram Figurine**: A ram figurine represents the Aries symbol and showcases its robust and fiery nature. This figurine may be worn close to the skin as an accessory.
- **Iron talisman (also known as "Mars Medallion")**: Mars, the ruling planet for Aries, is associated with the metal iron. Therefore, wearing or

carrying an iron symbol or talisman can heighten their courage and assertiveness.

- **Arrow symbol**: Represents Aries's direct, goal-oriented nature, reminding them to stay focused and driven.
- **Aina gemstone**: The Aina gemstone may be worn by Aries individuals for protection and courage.

• Your Daily Affirmations and Mantras (Chants):

As discussed previously in section 5.6. affirmations are positive, self-uplifting statements that people repeat to themselves to encourage a healthier mindset and boost self-confidence. They may be voiced aloud, penned down, or used for silent reflection to help individuals visualize and internalize positive thoughts and ideas about themselves and their goals. Research has shown that affirmative statements help reshape negative thought patterns by focusing on optimistic and constructive beliefs. We will look at examples of Aries-focused positive affirmations and mantras in the book's next chapter.

• Reflection and Gratitude Journaling:

A gratitude journal is simply a journal for documenting everything you are grateful for daily. It emphasizes positivity. It is different from a planner, diary, jot, or notebook. A gratitude journal records what you are grateful for in the present time. On the other hand, a planner is for writing what you plan or wish to do; a diary is for tracking everything (both good and bad) that have happened during the course of your day; a jot is for writing random important things that happened during the day which you would like to remember or follow up on;

and a notebook is just like a jot – for taking notes about present or future events and to help you remember important points that may require revisiting. Therefore, the gratitude journal, in comparison to the other items, is the only one dedicated to acknowledging and appreciating the positive events or occurrences in your life (Ackerman, 2017). One might ask why it matters to track the positive experiences in one's life. Multiple research investigations have shown that regularly identifying and writing down the good things in one's life daily is beneficial in many ways. An investigative research study of a three-month trial of gratitude journaling by O'Connell, O'Shea, & Gallagher (2017) revealed that among the study subjects, both reflective journaling (finding things to be grateful for) and reflective-behavioral journaling (finding things to be grateful for <u>and</u> expressing your gratitude) have a notable, positive impact on the participants' wellbeing, affect, and mood. Below are a few of the benefits of keeping a gratitude journal as an integral part of your daily self-care.

- Lowers stress level
- Eliminates insomnia
- Offers clarity on issues
- Keeps the writer's mindset on progress and achievements rather than failures
- Creates an opportunity for self-reflection and self-awareness
- Keeps the writer more mindful, helping he/she to become more grounded
- Helps visualize the bigger picture about life and living.

With the above advantages in mind, dear Aries, you should make a note to pick out an excellent inspirational journal book for your self-care gratitude journaling, if you haven't already done so.

Chapter 6

Chakra-Balancing Self-Care Plan for Aries

6.1 Why a chakra-balancing self-care plan?

This short chapter will discuss the purpose, benefits, and process of creating a chakra-balancing self-care plan for Aries, targeting the human body's seven main energy centers (chakras).

What is the rationale for creating a chakra-focused self-care plan, you may ask? Creating a chakras-centered, self-care plan for individuals born under the Aries zodiac sign can be a valuable tool for self-discovery and self-actualization. By understanding that the chakras play a critical role in maintaining a healthy and functioning body and mind, the Aries individual can take the necessary steps to balance and protect them by creating a comprehensive self-care plan based on sharpening the chakras. With healthy (unblocked) chakras in place, Aries individuals are empowered to utilize their subtle energy forces to enhance their naturally endowed beneficial attributes (boldness, assertiveness, and abundant energy) to generate positive outcomes in various aspects of their lives.

6.2 Root Chakra (Muladhara)

The Aries individual needs a solid and well-grounded Root Chakra (also known as the Base Chakra) to create a sturdy foundation for good health and for tending to the other chakras above the base. A solid root chakra will also help Aries manage specific inherent characteristics. For example, with an open, healthy, and solid root chakra, Aries can manifest their adventurous nature without being too impulsive.

Action steps: To achieve this:

- Include self-care activities in your daily routine (such as yoga exercises) that are calming and meditative. The Mountain Pose and the Warrior Pose are two root-reinforcing yoga poses that connect the spiritual body to Mother Earth.
- Spending time in nature (gardening, nature walking, bird watching, star gazing, hiking, and so on) or engaging in outdoor nature-embracing physical exercises (brisk walking, jogging, running, bicycling, yoga, work-out sessions, etc.) are reliable ways to strengthen the Root Chakra.
- Furthermore, mindfulness meditation exercises focused on safety, security, and stability can help Aries individuals feel more anchored in their Root/Base Chakras. For more effectiveness, we suggest including

targeted positive affirmations during these mindful meditation exercises.

6.3 Sacral Chakra (Svadhisthana)

The Sacral Chakra presides over an individual's creativity and emotional balance. Aries individuals have a natural aptitude for creativity. This innate skill makes them invaluable team members for projects that involve generating new ideas and thinking outside the box. A balanced Sacral Chakra is needed to release and use this creative side of their nature.

Action steps: To achieve this:

- Engage in activities that allow self-expression and serve as creative outlets for the mind. These activities include painting, drawing, dancing, graphic design, acting, songwriting, journaling, and other creative art forms.
- Regularly engage in activities that release your inner peace, joy, and passion. These activities help to strengthen and open the Sacral Chakra, creating a pathway for your subtle energy to flow through and thus increasing your grounding, creativity, and self-expression.
- Aries individuals could also benefit from soul-searching activities like journaling about feelings or trying new experiences that stimulate their senses. Journaling, for example, is an outlet to vent and release pent up emotions and thoughts that would otherwise be harmful to the psyche if left to fester

within. Taking it further, some people have turned their soul-baring journaling into writing careers that changed their lives completely.

6.4 Solar Plexus Chakra (Manipura)

Aries naturally have powerful Solar Plexus Chakras, which are associated with their confidence and leadership qualities. The Solar Plexus Chakra is the strongest chakra in all individuals born under the Aries zodiac constellation. Thus, bolstering the Solar Plexus Chakra can reinforce/fortify Aries's personal power. So, how would you boost the Solar Plexus Chakra?

Action steps: Here are some actions to take to boost and maintain a balanced Solar Plexus Chakra:

- Get involved in activities that bolster your self-esteem. This includes joining a debate club if you are a high school or college student, engaging in public speaking gigs, assuming or volunteering for leadership roles, etc.
- Core-strengthening exercises like yoga, Pilates, gymnastics, or martial arts can strengthen the Solar Plexus Chakra. Therefore, adding these exercises to your daily self-care routine would be a way to balance this chakra.
- Engaging in deep breathing exercises, verbalizing soul-uplifting mantras, and voicing positive affirmations centered on self-empowerment and physical strength are effective ways to strengthen this

chakra because these activities expand the chest cavity and, thus, the solar plexus.

6.5 Heart Chakra (Anahata)

Compassion is not a common virtue seen in Aries individuals. The Heart Chakra oversees compassion and love, two attributes that may often be overlooked or dismissed by the occasionally insensitive Aries personality. Needless to say, it is essential that Aries individuals seek ways to open up and balance their Heart Chakra.

Action steps: To address this, Aries must learn to balance self-love and love for others. Below are ways to achieve this.

- Therefore, they should consider activities like intercessory praying (praying for the good of others, that is, non-self-directed prayers), compassionate meditation, intercession meditation, or volunteering in the community to help open the Heart Chakra.
- Performing regular breathing exercises (breathwork) and soft (mellow) yoga exercises are heart-opening activities that balance and fortify the heart chakra.
- Engaging in social activities that deepen their connections with others is another option for Aries to facilitate an open and balanced Heart Chakra.

6.6 Throat Chakra (Vishuddha)

The Throat Chakra governs communication (speaking) abilities. Aries individuals have the tendency to be blunt/direct and speak impulsively. This communication style can rub others the wrong way. Therefore, devising ways to balance the Throat Chakra can enhance their communication skills.

Action steps: Here is how they can shore up their Throat Chakra.

- Encouraging activities that involve using your voice, such as ululating, yodeling, singing, chanting, humming, or engaging in measured conversations and open dialogues can help fortify the Throat Chakra. These activities engage and physically exercise the vocal cords, thus making them more resilient.
- Aries individuals can also keep a gratitude journal to articulate their thoughts and feelings. This helps to condense their impulsive thoughts into coherent, rational, and constructive conversations.
- Maintaining positive (optimistic) verbal communications rather than negative (pessimistic) verbal communication is another way to promote a balanced and open throat chakra.

6.7 Third Eye Chakra (Ajna)

Intuition, foresight, and emotional perception are not Aries's most impressive qualities. A well-balanced Third Eye Chakra is vital for enhancing Aries's intuitive ability.

Action steps: Here's what can be done to enhance the Third Eye Chakra:

- Practicing mindfulness meditation helps Aries to visualize and commit to their transitional goals (temporary/short-term goals) as well as their lifelong goals (permanent/long-term) goals. It also helps with mapping future aspirations.
- Practicing meditative journaling and contemplative thought analysis can help sharpen Aries's instincts and decision-making skills.

6.8 Crown Chakra (Sahasrara)

The Crown Chakra is committed to helping an individual achieve spiritual elevation and wisdom. When the Crown Chakra is open, well-developed, and balanced, the individual is able to rediscover their spiritual self and connect with their higher purpose in life.

Action steps: Here are ways to fortify the Crown Chakra.

- Practicing meditation and yoga exercises.
- Spending quiet moments by yourself to encourage spiritual awareness.
- Studying beliefs and practices that promote spiritual enlightenment.

By maintaining optimal chakra balance through the above-described self-care practices, Aries individuals can learn how to elevate themselves and maintain a harmonious balance in all areas of their lives. Table 6 below summarizes the above discussion in a compact, easy-to-read format.

Table 6: Summary of the seven chakras and their associations

Chakra	Influencing color	Element association	Sensory association	Endocrine gland association
Crown Chakra (Sahasrara)	**Violet** (or Gold)	Spirit	All the senses	Pineal gland
Brow Chakra (Third Eye) (Ajna)	**Deep Blue**	Spirit	Extra-Sensory Perception (ESP)	Pituitary gland
Throat Chakra (Vishuddha)	**Turquoise**	Ether (Akasha)	Hearing	Thyroid & Parathyroid glands
Heart Chakra (Anahata)	**Green** (or Pink)	Air	Touch	Thymus
Solar Plexus Chakra (Manipura)	**Yellow**	Fire	Sight	Pancreas
Sacral Chakra (Svadisthana)	**Orange**	Water	Taste	Adrenal glands
Base Chakra (Muladhara)	**Red**	Earth	Smell	Testes/Ovaries

Chapter 7

Career Pathways

7.1 Career Paths for Aries

When it comes to choosing a career, Aries frequently has the best pickings because the combination of their unique attributes is appealing to employers. Aries is known as an ambitious, high-energy, risk-taking, creative leader who is naturally suited for dynamic, trail-blazing, and fast-paced career paths. The Aries individual performs best in careers and positions that require taking the initiative and leading or mentoring others. Leadership comes naturally to them whether in the corporate world (as part of the management team), business arena (as part of the marketing or sales team), entrepreneurship (as business owners), military, or politics. They also do well in careers involving quick thinking and bold decisions, such as firefighting. Their aptitude for creativity, risk-taking, and ability to think outside the box makes them ideal for being in charge of new projects or trialing fresh, innovative ideas, as seen in high-tech companies. It is important to remember that Aries individuals have a strong desire to be recognized for their hard work, which makes sense because of their ambitious nature and desire for success.

7.2 Best Professions for Aries

Some of the best professions for Aries may be categorized as follows based on the specific personality trait or attribute at play (needed to be successful in the profession):

- **Creativity and Independence**: Entrepreneurship
  - Aries members who gravitate towards creativity and independence would make great entrepreneurs.

- **Strength, Courage, Energetic, assertiveness, and Discipline**: These traits are required for outdoor sports professions such as coaching, law enforcement, and the military, or indoor professions such as the culinary arts.
  - Those Aries whose prominent characteristics include strength, courage, high energy, assertiveness, and a preference for working within established rules and boundaries or controlled environments would feel at home in outdoor professions such as sports coaching, law enforcement, the military, and firefighting. They could also opt for indoor

- **Energetic and competitive**: Athletes and personal trainers.
  - Energetic Aries who crave competition would most likely want to be athletes, personal trainers, bodybuilders, race car drivers, and such.

- **High-energy, Adrenaline-craving, Quick-thinking, and Problem-solving skills:** These traits are most valuable for medical professions such as doctors (especially ER and Surgery), emergency medical professionals, and firefighters. Those Aries who love science and technology and demonstrate natural quick-thinking and problem-solving skills would make great engineers, ER doctors, surgeons, EMT professionals, and firefighters.

- **Charismatic and persuasive skills; people-oriented skills: Business professions such as sales and marketing, Politics,** or the hospitality industry.
  - Socially adept Aries are usually charismatic and do well around people. Such Aries would find success and fulfillment in politics, business sales and marketing, and the hospitality industry.

7.3 Which Career Speaks to You?

As a junior or senior in high school, deciding your future career is an essential and enormous task. The pressure is compounded by the fact that there are timelines and deadlines for making some of the decisions that would ultimately affect your future as an adult. This is when you need the most guidance from your parents, school counselors, zodiac signs, and, yes, your intuition too. You know what skills you are excellent at. You know what activities you love or enjoy doing. Trust your intuition and let it guide you, and with guidance and input from your school counselors and family, you should be able to make the best career choice for you.

For the established career professional reading this book, you may be experiencing stagnancy in your current career or perhaps a lack of fulfillment. You may even have wondered if your career is right for you. These may be red flags that you are not where you are supposed to be career-wise. This book may be the push you need to find the answers you seek. Take this opportunity to review the predominant Aries characteristics that you embody and use this to analyze the various career options that match your characteristics. With the Aries self-care tools studied so far in this book, you have the resources needed to create and live an optimal and fulfilled life or make necessary changes to redirect your career towards the right path to fulfillment.

Chapter 8

Love and Relationships

8.1 Influence of Aries Personality on Relationships

Romantic relationships change constantly. The personality type of each of the partners contributes significantly in one way or another to the success or failure of the relationship. It is therefore logical to surmise that the zodiac personalities of the partners in a relationship play prominent roles in the survival and longevity of the relationship.

Aries individuals bring their high-powered, hard-to-ignore personalities filled with infectious optimism to their romantic relationships. In these relationships, Aries is bold, confident, and often takes the lead. Their communication style is honest and straightforward, which can sometimes make their approach to love appear intense. Furthermore, they can be impatient and impulsive which could be misunderstood by their partner as being selfish. In spite of these personality snags, Aries individuals are known to be loyal and committed once they find the right match.

8.2 The role of Zodiac astrology in finding your ideal love match in today's modern dating scene

Finding the ideal romantic partner in this modern-day society is an uphill task, a feat by itself. In today's fast-paced, digitalized dating scene filled with apps, ecards, emojis, and memes, engaging in the traditional face-to-face contact to meet and vet potential romantic partners is considered obsolete. Therefore, many people are turning to zodiac astrology as a guide to help them identify compatible partners and navigate the complexities of romantic relationships. With so many dating apps filled with immense numbers of deceptive online profiles, astrology offers stability and control for online daters by providing a means to assess personality traits, emotional needs, and romantic compatibility beyond the online profiles posted in the apps. When people look through a dating profile, they can examine the relevant zodiac signs and quickly estimate whether they are compatible with the potential partners or not. This offers a unique and personalized option for finding a compatible partner without actually meeting the person face to face. For some people, astrology presents a way to sift through the overwhelming number of "profile matches" on dating apps by narrowing down choices based on the Zodiac signs that align well with their own. Think of it like a valuable pre-screen option which creates a sense of comfort and direction in the never-ending search for romantic connections.

Another reason why astrology is so appealing in modern-day dating lies in the fact that it is easy to access and can be seamlessly integrated into one's daily life with barely any interruption. Unlike traditional personality tests, which often involve lengthy and tedious questionnaires, astrology produces quick, immediate answers based on familiar Zodiac symbols that people readily recognize and identify with. Some of the valuable information obtained from astrology includes sun signs, characteristic behaviors, personality styles, and birth chart analyses, all of which can be used to predict subtle differences and peculiarities in communication style, emotional responses, and relationship dynamics between individuals. Many dating platforms and apps now include zodiac signs in their members' profiles. This recognizes and caters to the widespread interest and value that people place on astrological information these days. As a result, astrology has become a playful tool that adds excitement to the dating process and enables individuals to better understand themselves and their prospective romantic partners. Furthermore, potential couples often break the initial ice when getting to know one another by engaging in conversations involving the exchange of zodiac sign information, personality characteristics, and preferences.

8.3 The Aries Male's Ideal Zodiac Love Matches

Leo and **Sagittarius** make excellent romantic matches for Aries males because both signs bring the same adventurous and independent energy as Aries. Leo's outgoing personality understands and enjoys Aries' blunt and bold personality. Aries and Leo are ruled by the fire element, which gives both of them confidence, determination, and passion. This similarity in background creates a basis for a meaningful connection between the two zodiac signs. Leo has a natural charisma and enthusiasm for life which matches the spirited nature seen with Aries individuals. Both signs enjoy being the center of attention and appreciate loyalty, honesty, and candor in their relationship. This makes their relationship straightforward and uncomplicated because they understand each other. In this partnership, Leo is the stable, grounded, and rational partner while Aries is the adventurous and impulsive partner and keeps Leo from getting bored. Together, they bring the best out of each other.

Another fire sign, Sagittarius, is also compatible with Aries because they share a love for adventure, freedom, and new experiences. The Sagittarius female is optimistic and easy-going by nature, which make the Aries male feel liberated and unrestrained. This creates a relationship where both partners feel free with each other and unhindered to explore life fully. In addition, Aries has a persevering and determined nature that harmonizes well with Sagittarius' curiosity. This makes them an incredibly successful and unstoppable pair when they work together as a team. The Sagittarius female also helps the Aries male balance their impulsiveness with a broader, more philosophical, and restrained perspective. In return, Aries inspires Sagittarius to be proactive and steadfast in bringing their ideas and aspirations to fruition. Both Zodiac signs respect each other's need for independence in a relationship which provides Aries the freedom they crave.

8.4 The Aries Female's Ideal Zodiac Love Matches

The Gemini male makes a fantastic match for Aries females because they share a sense of adventure and curiosity. The bold and spontaneous Aries female meshes well with the playful and adaptable Gemini male. The Gemini man keeps his Aries woman intrigued and inspired with his clever intellect, quick wit, and constant flow of ideas. In contrast, the Aries woman demonstrates an intensity and decisiveness that the male Gemini admires immensely. Both signs enjoy social activities and excitement, so their relationship rarely faces dull moments. The Gemini is open-minded, which helps him handle the Aries female's passionate and sometimes impulsive nature. This dynamic allows Aries to lead while still embracing new ideas and perspectives naturally.

Similarly, the Aquarius male is exciting and smart, and therefore a mentally stimulating match for the Aries female. Both signs are independent and creative. Aquarius has a characteristic, progressive approach to life which meshes well with the pioneering spirit that the trail-blazing Aries is known for. In other words, Aquarius is forward-thinking and not afraid to try new things, a trait that is similar to Aries's enthusiastic and naturally curious tendency. These similarities create a meaningful and comfortable relationship between the two signs because they understand and respect each other. Again, the Aquarius individual is known for being unpredictable, unconventional, and not one to follow established rules and boundaries. This attribute keeps the Aries partner intrigued and engaged. At the same time, Aries has a direct approach to life without sugar-coating issues which serves as a much-needed reality check for Aquarius from time to time. Furthermore, Aquarius tends to be emotionally detached and occasionally needs to have some personal space, which works well with the Aries's desire for freedom to pursue their own goals and passions. In sum, the Aquarius male and Aries female share several complementary personality features that give their union a high success rate prediction.

8.5 Two Signs Compatible for Both Male and Female Aries

The following two Zodiac signs are compatible with both male and female Aries: Libra and Aries (i.e., another Aries).

- **Libra vs Aries**

With Libra, the relationship dynamic with Aries is based on an attraction between opposite personalities. Libra (symbolized by the weighing scale) is the zodiac sign for balance and harmony. This contrasts with the confident, bold brashness of the Aries bull-like personality. Surprisingly, a union of these two signs creates a complementary and intriguing match for both males and females. Aries has a bold and dominant style which differs from Libra's diplomatic, peace-loving nature. The result is an effective relationship where each partner balances out the weaknesses of the other.

Aries males, for instance, appreciate the Libra female's calmness, elegance, charm, and natural ability to promote harmony. These personality traits of the Libra female can tone down the impulsive and headstrong personality sometimes shown by the Aries male. The Libra female, on the other hand, finds Aries' confidence and direct approach exciting. She is often drawn to the Aries male's ability to make decisive choices, something Libra occasionally struggles with. This balance creates a strong relationship that allows Libra and Aries to support and learn from each other, with Libra teaching Aries patience and grace while Aries encourages Libra to embrace their inner strength and assertiveness.

For Aries females, Libra male partners offer stability and a sense of grounding that Aries often needs. The Libra male's calm demeanor and openness to dialogue conforms well with the Aries female's desire for honesty and rationality. The reserved and conservative Libra male is enthralled by the adventurous and impulsive side of the Aries female. In many ways, these two opposite personalities complement and strengthen each other instead of triggering conflict as one would expect.

- **Aries vs Aries**

This pair of similar personalities works. Surprised? Well, let's dive into this relationship situation to understand the dynamic. When two Aries come together in a romantic relationship, the result is an amplified connection because both partners have similar personalities and understand each other. They know how to stimulate each other and understand why they behave the way they do. There is a low learning curve compared to other unions because these two truly "get" each other. Occasional power struggles or competition may arise in this relationship because both parties are natural leaders who love to take charge. However, the fact that both Aries understand and respect each other's need for independence can create a strong foundation for mutual trust. For this pair, their romance is authentic and thrives because they are compatible in being spontaneous, adventurous, and enthusiastic in everything they do. On the other hand, both will likely need to work on compromise and patience to avoid clashes. When balanced, this partnership could become an inspiring and successful union for both partners.

Chapter 9

Practical Tips and Advice

9.1 Sample Daily Affirmations and Mantras (Chants) for Aries

Below are thirty-one (31) carefully selected, powerful, Aries-focused positive affirmations that you may include in your daily self-care regimen. Focus on one positive affirmation daily for one month, with each day's affirmation accompanied by breathwork meditation using crystals and daily journaling. You will be amazed at the effect on every area of your life.

1. I am a natural-born leader.
2. I embrace my inner strength.
3. I lead with confidence, clarity, and consideration for others.
4. I lead by example and with purpose.
5. I inspire others with my courage and determination.
6. I am fierce and fearless.

7. I pursue my dreams with passion.
8. I trust in my ability to succeed today and every day.
9. I embrace my individuality and independence.
10. I embrace my fierce independence and also value my connections and relationships.
11. My passion fuels me. It does not control me.
12. I thrive in action and lead with positivity.
13. I am bold; I can take on any challenge that comes my way.
14. I am strong; I am designed to overcome difficulties.
15. I am courageous; Problems will not defeat me.
16. I believe in ME; I trust my ability to succeed.
17. I am bold, I am adventurous, I am exciting
18. I am bold; I am adventurous; I make things happen.
19. I love people; I will be kind and respectful with my words.
20. I am focused; I am driven; I am an achiever!
21. I am focused on my goals, and I will not be distracted.
22. I trust my instincts and am not afraid to take the initiative.
23. I believe in my dreams and trust my ability to make them come true.
24. I am resilient; I can recover from every setback.
25. If I fall today, I will rise to be better.
26. I am in control; My emotions do not rule me.
27. I will start and end today with a calm mind.
28. I release impatience and embrace composure.
29. I am optimistic; I see the good in all situations.
30. Everyone I see today will have a reason to smile.
31. My energy is positive; My thoughts are optimistic.

9.2 Biblical Support for Astrology

This book purposes to stimulate a desire for self-awareness and empowerment for Aries individuals through positive, zodiac-based self-care. Its intent is not to critique, dissect, or judge any religion. That said, it has been noted that there is a general belief that the Bible (Christianity) and astrology are incompatible. Because of this, I deemed it necessary to provide evidence of Biblical mention and approval of astrology to reassure our Christian readers.

The story of Jesus's birth is a pinnacle of the Christian faith. The New Testament book of Matthew, Chapter 2, tells the story of the astrological and political circumstances surrounding his birth. Jesus was born in Bethlehem, a small Judean town in Jerusalem, to ordinary immigrant parents who had traveled to Bethlehem because of a census that the then-Roman Emperor Caesar Augustus ordered. This census order required everyone to register in their ancestral hometown. Joseph (Jesus' father), a descendant of King David's lineage, was required to travel to his hometown, Bethlehem, to register for the census, with his fiancé Mary who was pregnant at the time. This was during the reign of King Herod the Great over the land of Judea.

Fun Fact: Brief historical background of Judea at the time of Jesus' birth

During this historical period, the Roman Empire conquered and occupied Jewish provincial cities, including Judea. The position of the King of Judea at that time was not hereditary but rather filled by appointment from Rome. In this case, King Herod the Great of Judea was appointed by the Roman Emperor Caesar Augustus. Herod was considered a "puppet king" with limited powers because the ultimate political power over the region resided with their Roman conquerors.

The chapter reveals that astrological constellations in the heavens (skies)had predicted Jesus' unique birth and the critical role he would play in the world. It goes on to state that three wise men (astrologers) from the East (present-day East Asia) had noted and charted the unique placement of the zodiac constellations at the time of his birth and correctly recognized that the pattern indicated a unique personality. The significance of this finding was so enormous and vital that they set out to locate the child whose extraordinary birth had been predicted. Upon arrival in Jerusalem, the three astrologers (also referred to as "The Magi" in various texts) sought information from the locals that would lead them to the birth location and parents of Jesus. They told the local people that they were trying to find a child whose birth had been predicted by the stars as a future leader and savior of the Jews and the world. Unfortunately, their arrival and peculiar questions were brought to the attention of King Herod, who became apprehensive and fearful of the birth of a potential political opponent who could usurp his political position by raising opposition among the people. To preserve his rulership and kingdom, King Herod cunningly welcomed the three astrologers, hosted them lavishly, provided them with supplies, and asked them to let him know as soon as they found the baby Jesus so that he too could come to honor and welcome him into the world as a future leader. Herod's true intention, however, was to obtain the information about the newborn child so that he could eliminate that future threat. Unfortunately, his plans were thwarted because after the astrologers found Jesus and presented him with three spiritu-ally significant gifts (gold, frankincense, and myrrh), they received a spiritual warning during sleep meditation about the evil intentions of King Herod. An angel guided them to return home using a different route to avoid the King (see the Bible's New Testament Book of Matthew, Chapter 2, verses 1-23). (*Holy Bible (NIV)*, 2008).

Several salient points from the above story indicate that Christianity recognizes and accepts the legitimacy and impor-tance of astrology as a crucial part of human existence.

- First, it is significant that "star gazing" and interpretation of the constellations existed millions of years ago BC (Before Christ).

- Astrological predictions were welcomed rather than shunned or feared during Christ's time. This statement is supported by the fact that astrologers from the Far East openly explained who they were and their mission, and they were welcomed and treated well by the people of Jerusalem at the time. That would not have happened if their profession was considered taboo.

- Similarly, Joseph and Mary, Jesus' parents, welcomed these Eastern visitors with open arms. They hosted them graciously and accepted the predictions about their newborn child and the unique gifts they brought to honor him. It is unlikely that Joseph and Mary would have welcomed three strangers with scary predictions about their newborn child if they did not believe in the legitimacy of their profession and predictions.

- Reviewing the spiritual importance of these three gifts shows that they were specifically selected to mark three essential aspects of Jesus' life (Basilica, 2020):

  1. **Gold**: *Kingship*. The Magi's gift of gold signifies Jesus's kingship, royalty, leadership, and elevated spiritual status. This supports the prediction that Jesus would be a spiritual leader and savior of Jewish people and all believers.

  2. **Frankincense**: *Deity*. In the Old Testament Jewish laws, the herb frankincense was traditionally burned in the Jewish temple by the High Priest as an offering to God on behalf of the people. Gifting Jesus

frankincense signified his divinity, and the ritualistic burning of the frankincense emphasized his future role as both the holy High Priest and the future sacrificial offering to God in exchange for the cleansing and redemption of all believers.

3. **Myrrh**: *Death*. Myrrh was a ubiquitous embalming agent during the time of Christ. Its primary use was for preserving dead bodies, and it was not considered a typical baby gift during that era. The gift of myrrh by the three wise men foretold Jesus' death. It is also noted later in the Book of John, Chapter 19, verses 38-40, that the disciple Nicodemus brought myrrh at the time of Jesus' burial to be used for embalming his body:

"…Nicodemus, the one who had first come to him (Jesus) at night, also came bringing a mixture of myrrh and aloes weighing about one hundred pounds. They took the body of Jesus and bound it with burial cloths along with the spices, according to the Jewish burial custom." (John 19:38-40)

- After visiting with Jesus, the three Magi were warned by an angel in a dream-like vision about the evil intentions of King Herod and were subsequently guided home via a different route to evade the King. The fact that angels (recognized and accepted spiritual guides by Christians) communicated to the Magi through psychic methods as a means to save

Jesus' life underscores the acceptance of psychic communication (a part of astrology) by the Christian faith.

In conclusion, Biblical evidence shows that zodiac constellation interpretation (astrology) and psychic dream interpretation were recognized and accepted during Jesus' era and should not be dismissed or maligned as evil by modern-day Christians.

Fun fact:

The word "Magi" (singular "Magus") is a derivative of the Latin word of the same spelling, which translates as "Persian Priest" or "Persian wise man," and from the Greek word "Magos," meaning "Persian Priest" or "Persian Sorcerer."

9.3 Bible Verses for the Aries Personality

Having hopefully dispelled any fears or concerns our Christian readers may have had, let us dive into Bible passages that address specific Aries's needs for daily self-care.

Aries individuals are known for possessing traits like enthusiasm, fearlessness, leadership, and determination. As part of their daily self-care, Aries individuals would benefit from Bible verses that complement their personality traits and encourage them to channel their passion and boundless energy in positive ways. Here are ten selected Bible passages that address specific Aries personality traits and are curated to inspire, support, and nurture their unique personalities.

1. Joshua 1:9 – Courage and Strength

"Have I not commanded you? Be strong and courageous. Do not be afraid; do not be discouraged, for the Lord your God will be with you wherever you go."

This verse is from the Book of Joshua in the Old Testament of the Holy Bible and speaks to Aries's inborn bravery and leadership qualities. It encourages Aries to be bold in everything they do and to trust that God will see them through every challenge they face now and in the future. This Bible verse will make an excellent positive daily affirmation for Aries's self-care.

2. Proverbs 28:1 – Fearlessness

"The wicked flee though no one pursues, but the righteous are as bold as a lion."

Aries individuals often exhibit fearless courage. This verse compares righteous boldness to that of a lion, a symbol of strength, which corresponds with Aries's innate desire to act fearlessly. It is noteworthy that a pre-condition for this boldness is "righteousness." The implication is that God approves boldness predicated on doing the right thing, that is, boldness for the common good. For example, boldly speaking up to bring attention to policy violations at your workplace is righteous boldness and encouraged. Conversely, boldly and brazenly violating policy or cutting corners is not encouraged because it is not for the common good; it is not positive boldness.

3. Romans 12:11 – Passion and Zeal

"Never be lacking in zeal, but keep your spiritual fervor, serving the Lord."

Aries are known for their passionate nature, and this verse encourages them to channel their zeal into serving others and maintaining their spiritual enthusiasm. According to New Testament Biblical principles, "serving the Lord" is like saying "serving others" because the teachings of Jesus are based on the premise that you see and love others as God sees and loves you. In this passage, therefore, Aries individuals are encouraged to be as conscientious in serving others as they are in serving God. In other words, channel your zeal (passion and fervor) into doing good for the benefit of humanity.

4. 1st Timothy 4:12 – Leadership

"Don't let anyone look down on you because you are young, but set an example for the believers in speech, in conduct, in love, in faith and in purity."

As we have discussed throughout this journey, Aries is a natural-born leader. This verse emphasizes the leadership role that young people should aspire for. It encourages the young Aries to lead by example through their actions and faith. It is the only way people will trust and believe in you. Always let your actions speak for you.

5. Philippians 4:13 – Perseverance

"I can do all this through Him who gives me strength."

This Bible verse is a popular favorite and would make an excellent daily positive affirmation or mantra. Aries individuals are known for their ability to easily overcome challenges. This verse is an inspiration to Aries because it reminds them to rely on God's strength when going through stressful circumstances. Powerful verses like this can effectively channel positive energies during mindful meditation practices.

6. Isaiah 40:31 – Energy and Endurance

"But those who hope in the Lord will renew their strength. They will soar on wings like eagles; they will run and not grow weary; they will walk and not be faint."

Even the innately enthusiastic and energetic Aries can run out of gas sometimes. This verse is designed for the weary and depleted Aries who may be having a bad day or a frustrating week. This Old Testament Bible verse reminds them that with God's support, they can remain optimistic even in the most trying times.

7. Proverbs 3:5-6 – Trust in God's Plan

"Trust in the Lord with all your heart and lean not on your own understanding; in all your ways submit to him, and he will make your paths straight."

Humility, caution, and contemplation are not the most robust virtues for most Aries. As discussed previously, Aries can sometimes be impulsive and headstrong in their daily lives and dealings with others. This Bible verse encourages them to be humble, submissive, and trusting of God's guidance, even when driven to act independently.

8. James 1:19 – Patience and Temperance

"My dear brothers and sisters, take note of this: Everyone should be quick to listen, slow to speak and slow to become angry."

Aries can be prone to quick reactions and impulsive anger, which could impede their social relationships over time. This Bible verse gently encourages them to practice patience and listen carefully.

9. Matthew 5:16 – Leading by Example

"In the same way, let your light shine before others, that they may see your good deeds and glorify your Father in heaven."

Leadership is a responsibility. As natural leaders, Aries are often in the spotlight and expected to perform well. This verse encourages them to use their leadership for good and to inspire others by living exemplary lives that model their beliefs.

10. Ephesians 6:10 – Strength in Faith

"Finally, be strong in the Lord and in His mighty power."

Aries are known and admired for their strength and determination. This Bible verse reminds them to draw strength from

God and encourages them to continuously seek to increase their spiritual knowledge and faith.

To summarize dear Aries, the above scriptural verses were selected to reflect your personality and showcase the attributes that make you special. They are meant to remind you to be humble and embrace your natural-born and God-approved courage. Through the Holy Scriptures and your self-care tools, you can utilize your strengths and challenges in ways that glorify God, maintain your inner peace, and positively impact others. Be sure to memorize and pull up these words of encouragement and nuggets of wisdom whenever you need exhortation or when you feel down and need emotional support. For example, when tempted to be impulsive or succumb to quick temper or reactionary response to a situation, pull up James 1:19 in your mind's eye and take a step back to meditate on the message in that verse. Use the opportunity to weigh on the benefits of patience and temperance versus impatience and lack of self-control. Repeat this affirmation: "I am in control; My emotions do not rule me." Continue to meditate as you listen for any spiritual guidance that comes to you. You are born to succeed.

9.4 Maintaining Your Self-Care as An Aries: The Importance of Routine and Commitment

A regular self-care routine allows individuals to address their mental, emotional, and physical health proactively. The same is true for Aries. Keeping a regular schedule of self-care activities reduces stress and prevents burnout for high-energy zodiac signs such as Aries. The challenge, however, lies in maintaining the routine over time. Routine and commitment are crucial to maintaining daily self-care because they create structure and consistency, which are pertinent factors to long-term well-being. Committing to self-care practices helps Aries individuals stay mindful and aware of their needs, especially during strenuous times. The first step in the commitment process to self-care is prioritizing it.

By nature of their ruling planet (Mars) and their fire element which enhance their go-getter personality, Aries individuals are especially susceptible to burnout if they do not prioritize self-care. For Aries to maintain an effective self-care routine, they require structure, self-discipline, and a commitment to balancing their high-energy lifestyle with a designated time for rest and renewal. Furthermore, to be effective, Aries's self-care routine should not limit their natural impulses but rather enhance or downplay them as needed over the long term.

Here are ten practical tips for staying committed to your Aries self-care regimen.

1. **Set Clear, Achievable Goals**: Start with small, realistic self-care practices and gradually build from there. You do not have to begin with all the self-care tools at once in the beginning. Making the goals achievable means realistically setting self-care goals within the realm of possibility. Do not sabotage your efforts by overwhelming yourself from the beginning by setting unrealistic goals. Furthermore, aim to set clear goals because they make it easier to stay motivated.

2. **Schedule Your Self-Care Time**: Treat your self-care routine like an appointment by setting aside dedicated time in your daily or weekly schedule and sticking to it.

3. **Create a Routine You Enjoy**: Choose activities you genuinely enjoy, such as singing or reciting a mantra, reading positive affirmations aloud, practicing mindfulness meditation with your favorite background music, or incorporating yoga stretches and exercises you like. Doing these will make self-care feel fun and rewarding rather than being a chore.

4. **Track Your Progress**: I encourage you to use a journal or app to track your self-care habits. This can help you see progress and maintain consistency. For most people, seeing progress reinforces commitment. It can also help you see weak areas that need readjustment or prioritization.

5. **Stay Flexible**: Remain flexible as much as your lifestyle permits. Allow room for adjustment of your self-care schedule. If life gets busy, modify your self-care routine to fit your current needs rather than skipping it entirely.

6. **Seek Accountability from Yourself and Others**: Hold yourself accountable for failures or mishaps without guilt-tripping. Share your self-care goals with a friend or partner, or join a group focused on well-being so you have someone to encourage and support your efforts. Sharing your self-care journey with another person or a group is a powerful motivator. You may also consider getting a wellness/life coach or mentor.

7. **Commemorate Your Small Successes and Large Milestones**: Acknowledge any achievements/milestones and reward yourself for sticking with your routine, even if it is just completing a single self-care activity for the day. Go all out to highlight and rejoice over your success in meeting significant commitment milestones.

8. **Make Yourself a Priority**: Remember that self-care is not selfish but essential. Commit to making your well-being a priority in your daily life.

9. **Be Prepared in Advance**: Set up everything you need for your self-care activities beforehand so it is easier to follow through without excuses. Preparation reduces the chances of failure and discouragement.

10. **Review and Reflect**: Regularly re-assess your personal self-care plan to see how your routine is working. Reflect on what makes you feel best and adjust your self-care practices as needed. I recommend daily reflection on your progress as part of your gratitude journaling at the end of each self-care routine.

There you go, Aries! I hope you find some or all of these tips helpful. Your self-care journey may be rough initially, but rest assured that over time, you will begin to look forward to your self-care moments, appreciating that they are necessary for living your best life in your zodiac realm.

Chapter 10

Aries in a Nutshell

This final chapter in our journey summarizes all the fantastic things we have learned about Aries into one easy-to-read table for quick referencing. I hope you enjoy reading and referencing it as much as I enjoyed compiling it for you!

10.1 Aries in a Nutshell

Your Zodiac Sign Dates:	March 21 – April 19
Your Symbol:	The Ram
Your Spirit Animal(s):	Cheetah; Hawk/Falcon
Your Nature Element:	Fire
Your Ruling Planet:	Mars
Your Prominent Personality:	Bold, Assertive, Confident, Charismatic, Creative

Your Compatible Pet(s): German Shepherd, Doberman,

Your Power Color: Red

Your Sunstones/Birthstones: Ruby and Diamond,

Your Sunstone/Birthstone Alternatives: Bloodstone and Sapphire

Your Signature Essential Oils: Rosemary

Your Herb/Essential Oil (Restorative): Black pepper, Ginger, Rosemary

Your Herb/Essential Oil (Calming/Soothing): Bergamot, German chamomile, Roman chamomile, Geranium

Your Best Career Choices: Entrepreneur; Corporate CEO/CFO; Corporate Team Leader; Athlete; Military; Law Enforcement; Firefighter; ER Doctor; Nurse Administrator, Chief Medical Officer, Chief Nursing Officer; Sales/Marketing Executive

Best Love Match (**for Male Aries**): Libra & Aries) **Leo** female; **Sagittarius** female; (also

Best Love Match (**for Female Aries**): Libra & Aries) **Gemini** male; **Aquarius** male; (also

Your Lucky Number (s): 9, 7, 17

Your Daily Mantra: "I am a trailblazer; I have the passion and purpose to create my own path."

"I am BOLD; I am STRONG; I have the courage to overcome all challenges"

Your Bible Affirmation: Philippians 4:13 "I can do all things through Him who strengthens me"

Your Personality Strengths: Bold, Strong, Charismatic, Assertive, Leader, Energetic, Enthusiastic, Proactive, Quick-thinking, Decisive, Adventurous; Competitive

Your Personality Challenges: Anger, Headstrong/Stubbornness, Aggression, Depression, Selfish, Outspoken/Direct, Impulsive

10.2 A Day in the Life of an Aries

Below is a personal self-care regimen shared by an Aries friend and client who is invested in self-care. I hope you can gain some guidance from her lifestyle.

My name is Aaliyah, and I am an Aries. I was born on April 19th. My name was chosen with intention by my parents because it means "highly elevated," "most exalted one," and "influential leader." My journey to self-care and self-empowerment began 2 years ago. I realized soon after graduating from nursing school and working at the local trauma center in my community that something was missing from my life. On the surface, it appeared as though I had everything: a great profession that I loved, a great job and employer, amazing co-workers, a lovely house in a nice neighborhood, and caring family and friends. However, I knew something was missing beneath the surface because my spirit was restless. I knew that I needed something more to achieve self-fulfillment and self-actualization. I am an avid reader and book collector. One day, while browsing books on Amazon, I chanced across an interesting-looking book on astrology by an author I had never heard of. I looked up her profile on Amazon and found that she had a background on the topic and that people loved her books. I purchased the book, and my life was never the same again.

From that book, I learned about myself, my zodiac history, and how a better understanding of my astrological self (zodiac sign and natal pattern) could lead to a more fulfilling life. I first needed to get my natal chart (birth chart), which was easy to order through a reputable online astrologer. Studying my birth chart provided clarity on the nuances of my character and personality. From the chart, I learned the position of the sun and planets at the specific time of my birth. I also learned about aspects, chart patterns, chart houses, astrological angles, the influence of inner and outer planets, and so on. I connected with an astrologer who helped with the interpretations and eventually became my personal astrologer and advisor. Most importantly, I learned how to utilize all the information I had gathered about the subtleties of my personality to create a lifestyle explicitly tailored for me. I am going to share a brief snapshot of that lifestyle with you.

My home is a three-bedroom family house in a suburban neighborhood. Before that, I had lived in a small apartment in the city, so I can confidently tell you that the location and size of your home should not hinder your self-care practices in any way. Regarding the environmental aspect of my self-care practices, the front porch and flower beds surrounding my home are decorated with my favorite potted herb plants, selected specifically for their compatibility with my zodiac sign, Aries. These include thyme, ginger, and peppermint. Their soothing and refreshing fragrances fill the air as you walk up the porch steps to the front door. The front door opens into a small foyer. I placed one Aries abundance stone (Carnelian) inconspicuously on opposite sides of the foyer entranceway to attract good fortune and wealth to the household. The furnishings and décor in every room have shades of ruby red incorporated into them. I have a few more potted herbs placed decoratively at window ledges in the kitchen and the backyard. My birthstones (Ruby and Diamond) are placed strategically in commonly used areas of my home. They are also incorporated into the décor. In addition, I have a unique large ruby stone that I keep under my pillow while I sleep. (Note: You may substitute a bloodstone for a ruby if needed).

For the personal aspect of my self-care regimen, I begin the day with a prayer and recitation of my selected mantra, followed by a 10-minute breathing exercise with my ruby sunstone in my hand. I perform the recitations and breathing exercises in sets of 7 or 9 because both are lucky numbers for Aries. I wear a ruby or diamond necklace, bracelet, and/or earrings every day. As I prepare for the day, I set my intentions and recite my designated affirmation(s) for the day. I continue to meditate on the words of my affirmations or mantra throughout the day's activities, including during my commute and at work. I have recordings of my daily mantras playing in the car as I commute throughout the day. I keep a piece of raw carnelian stone (my abundance stone) in the purse I carry, and I have another piece of carnelian placed at a corner of my office desk to attract good fortune and wealth. Back home at the end of the day, I shower with my lavender-infused soap and wash my hair with peppermint-infused shampoo to benefit from its refreshing and mental acuity sharpening prop-erties. I have my daily mindfulness meditation sessions sched-uled for nighttime so that I can take my time and enjoy the session without any pressure. I hold these sessions in a quiet, designated room in the house, and I always begin the sessions with a breathing exercise while holding my favorite diamond or ruby stone in my hand. I like to meditate on my intentions for the next day, written on paper and placed under a ruby crystal within my view and touch. Occasionally, when I can invite a friend for the session, I use the opportunity to hold a chakra cleansing and balancing ritual with them. My evening meditation typically lasts about 15-20 minutes, and it ends with the positive-affirmation recital. At bedtime, I sleep with my favorite birthstone under my pillow.

Finally, the pertinent point to remember in self-care is that there is no standardized method or recipe. It is a lifestyle, not a robotic routine. My personal lifestyle described above works for me. It is shared simply to show how I have incorporated many of the available Aries resources into my life. It is not a recipe or blueprint that you must copy. The objective is for you to use this as a template and modify and adjust it to suit you. Once you know all your Aries power resources (which we have discussed extensively in this book), it is up to you to utilize this framework to create a routine that is perfect for you.

Afterword

Congrats, Aries! We have come to the end of this exciting journey! As we wrap up *Zodiac Self-Care Guide: Aries*, I hope that you have learned a lot and, most importantly, that you have enjoyed the entire discovery process. Throughout the discussions over the last ten chapters, it was emphasized that understanding yourself and nurturing your unique qualities are the keys to a balanced and fulfilling life. From exploring and understanding the core traits and celestial influences that mold your identity to discovering self-care practices designed explicitly for your courageous and adventurous spirit, this book was crafted to guide you in taking advantage of your inborn strengths as an Aries while helping you mitigate your weaknesses. You have learned not only what makes you who you are but also the tools that support your personal growth and how to use them to nourish your mind, body, and spirit. The book was divided into two parts: Part one (self-study) and part two (self-care).

In part one of the book, you gained a better understanding of your personality by analyzing the individual bricks that make up the foundation of your identity as an Aries. The concept of self-awareness (self-study) as the first step in Aries' self-care was the focal point of the discussion in part one. For Aries, this is incredibly empowering, as it allows you to harness your remarkable energy, determination, and courage while also learning to pause and nurture yourself. The section began with an introduction of astrology as the basis of the Zodiac system. Astrology was differentiated from astronomy, and a comprehensive explanation of the constellations and the Zodiac System was presented. Next, the significance of the ram as the symbolic representation of Aries was explained. The conversation topic continued in chapter two on the four natural elements and how the fire element influences the Aries' personality. A deep dive into the celestial elements, including the influences of the sun, moon, and the Aries' ruling planet, Mars, was conducted in chapter three. Part One concluded with an in-depth analysis of the characteristics, strengths, and common challenges Aries faced and how to overcome them. In Part Two, you discovered the various resources available to you, Aries, for self-care and learned how to use them. You also received guidelines and tips for choosing your career and romantic partners wisely based on your specific personality type and unique characteristics as Aries.

In conclusion, it was made clear during this journey that embracing who you are begins with understanding the peculiar celestial influences that define your characteristics and mold your personality. By exploring the building blocks of your Aries personality, you gained insights into what drives

you and what constitutes your innate strengths. You also identified areas where you may need balance and self-care. You
now understand that self-care for Aries is more than just a
routine. It is not just a one-time practice session but a commitment to finding and retaining a balance between your inner
passion and periods of nurturing, rest, and reflection. This can
be achieved by embracing your power colors, incorporating
healing crystals that vibrate with the same energy as your
Zodiac sign, and connecting with your natural elements,
bringing a more profound sense of harmony to your life. Each
part of this book, from self-study to self-care, has provided you
with tools and guidance to navigate life as an Aries, with
particular attention to balancing your unparalleled fire-
inspired, Mars-driven traits. From grounding your root chakra
to focusing on your ambitions and maintaining balanced
personal and work relationships, these self-care practices are
tailored to help you thrive in every area of life. By practicing
the relaxation techniques, affirmations, and mindful
approaches shared in this book, you can remain firmly
grounded and resilient in a world full of daily challenges. This
journey is only the beginning of a beautiful and fulfilling life
ahead. You are encouraged to use the insights and practices
from this book to create a life that fully encapsulates and
showcases your bold, courageous, and passionate essence as an
Aries. As you move forward, remember that the best version
of yourself emerges when you are correctly aligned with the
energy that makes you uniquely you. So, let this guide remind
you to channel your energy mindfully, balance your intense
passions with moments of peace, and stay grounded in your
own truth. May you continue to grow, love, and pursue your
dreams with the confidence and resilience that make you

uniquely Aries.

[If you enjoyed this book or learned a thing or two from it, please leave a review to encourage others]

Bibliography

Ackerman, C. (2017). *Gratitude Journal: 67 Templates, Ideas, and Apps for Your Diary*. Positive Psychology. https://positivepsychology.com/gratitude-journal/

American Astronomical Society (n.d.). *What's the difference between astronomy and astrology?* |Aas.org. https://aas.org/faq/whats-difference-between-astronomy-and-astrology#:~:text=Astronomers%20base%20their%20studies%20on

American Psychological Association. (2019). "Mindfulness Meditation: A Research-Proven Way to Reduce Stress." *American Psychological Association*, 30 Oct. 2019, www.apa.org/topics/mindfulness/meditation.

Arroyo, Stephen (2012). Astrology, Psychology and the Four Elements: An Energy Approach to Astrology & Its Use in the Counselling Arts. Motilal Banarsidass Publ. ISBN 9788178223872

Astrology and the Elements: Earth, Air, Fire and Water Signs Meaning - My Framer Site. (n.d.). Www.thenightsky.com. https://www.thenightsky.com/blog/astrology-and-the-elements

Basilica. (2020). *What the Gifts of the Magi Tell Us about Jesus*. Basilica of the National Shrine of the Immaculate Conception. https://www.nationalshrine.org/blog/what-the-gifts-of-the-magi-tell-us-about-jesus/

Battaglia, S. (2022, August 25). *Aries: Astrological Aromatherapy*. Perfect Potion. https://www.perfectpotion.com.au/blogs/blog/aries-astrological-aromatherapy

Bergamot: Uses, Side Effects, Interactions, Dosage, and Warning. (2019). Webmd.com. https://www.webmd.com/vitamins/ai/ingredientmono-142/bergamot

Black, D. S., & Slavich, G. M. (2016). Mindfulness meditation and the immune system: a systematic review of randomized controlled trials. *Annals of the New York Academy of Sciences, 1373*(1), 13–24. https://doi.org/10.1111/nyas.12998

Breathwork for Beginners: What to Know and How to Get Started. (2024). Cleveland Clinic. https://health.clevelandclinic.org/breathwork

Brennan, D. (2021). "What Is Mindfulness Meditation?" *WebMD*. www.webmd.com/balance/what-is-mindfulness-meditation.

Brittanica. (2024). "Aries | Behind the Zodiac | Britannica." *Encyclopædia*

Britannica, 2024, www.britannica.com/video/this-month-in-astrology-Aries-Zodiac/-299742. Accessed 7 Oct. 2024.

Bubala, M. (2011). The Earth Has Shifted; The Zodiac Signs Have Changed. *CBS News, Baltimore.* https://www.cbsnews.com/baltimore/news/the-earth-has-shifted-the-zodiac-signs-have-changed/

Cascio, Christopher N., et al. "Self-Affirmation Activates Brain Systems Associated with Self-Related Processing and Reward and Is Reinforced by Future Orientation." *Social Cognitive and Affective Neuroscience*, vol. 11, no. 4, 5 Nov. 2015, pp. 621–629, https://doi.org/10.1093/scan/nsv136.

Cleveland Clinic. (n.d.). *King of the Jungle: How and Why to Practice Lion's Breath.* https://health.clevelandclinic.org/lions-breath

Cosmopolitan (2024). *Outspoken, Daring, and Bold? Say Hello to These 50 Celebrity Aries.* Cosmopolitan Online Magazine. https://www.cosmopolitan.com/entertainment/celebs/g35217933/famous-aries-celebrities/

Fincham, G. W., Strauss, C., Montero-Marin, J., & Cavanagh, K. (2023). Effect of Breathwork on Stress and Mental health: a meta-analysis of random-ized-controlled Trials. *Scientific Reports*, *13*(1). https://doi.org/10.1038/s41598-022-27247-y

Goldman, R. (2022). "Affirmations: What They Are and How to Use Them." *EverydayHealth.com.* Www.everydayhealth.com/emotional-health/what-are-affirmations/

Grof (n.d.). *About Holotropic Breathwork®.* Grof Transpersonal Training. https://www.holotropic.com/holotropic-breathwork/about-holotropic-breathwork/

Hall, J. (2005). *The Astrology Bible: The definitive guide to the zodiac.* Sterling Pub. Co.

Hall, J. (2004). *The Crystal Zodiac: Use birthstones to enhance your life.* Godsfield Press, a division of Octopus Publishing Group Ltd.

Hall, J. (2003). *The Crystal Bible.* Walking Stick Press.

Hall, M. (2014). *All Signs Have a Dark Side. What is Aries?* LiveAbout. https://www.liveabout.com/dark-side-of-aries-206454#:~:text=Aries%20of%20both%20sexes%20are

Healthline. (2018). *Bergamot Oil Uses and Benefits.* https://www.healthline.com/health/bergamot-oil

Healthline. (2023). *Breathwork Meditation: Benefits, Exercises, and Tips.* https://www.healthline.com/health/breath-work-meditation#benefits

Holy Bible (NIV). (2008). Zondervan.

Ilana, R. (2021, March 19). *Essential Oils for Your Astrological Sign: Aries.* The Essential Oil Company. https://www.essentialoil.com/blogs/news/essential-oils-for-your-astrological-sign-aries?srsltid=

AfmBOopOrITDRP3rbRMWi7LH2pzCUFUXIwn3SlmJhl7EyN3gVRn J7hzM

Institute for Integrative Nutrition. (2024). *Mantras vs. Affirmations: What's the Difference?* https://www.integrativenutrition.com/blog/2016/08/mantras-vs-affirmations-what-s-the-difference

Jocelyn, J. (1991). *Meditations On the Signs of the Zodiac.* Steiner Books.

Khoury, B. et al. (2013). "Mindfulness-Based Therapy: A Comprehensive Meta-Analysis." *Clinical Psychology Review*, vol. 33, no. 6, Aug. 2013, pp. 763–771, https://doi.org/10.1016/j.cpr.2013.05.005.

Lunar and Planetary Institute (n.d.). *Sky Tellers - Constellations.* https://www.lpi.usra.edu/education/skytellers/constellations/#:~:text=A%20constella-tion%20is%20a%20group

Melody. (1995). *Love Is in the Earth: A Kaleidoscope of Crystals.* Earth-Love Publishing House.

Mendillo, M. (2022). The Christianized Zodiac of the Northern Hemisphere. In: Saints and Sinners in the Sky: Astronomy, Religion and Art in Western Culture. Springer Praxis Books. Springer, Cham. https://doi.org/10.1007/978-3-030-84270-3_4

Mercier, P. (2007). *The chakra bible: the definitive guide to working with chakras.* Sterling.

Merriam-Webster. (2019). *Definition of SALUTOGENESIS.* Merriam-Webster.com. https://www.merriam-webster.com/dictionary/salutogenesis

Merriam-Webster. (2024). *Definition of AROMATHERAPY.* Www.merriam-Webster.com. https://www.merriam-webster.com/dictionary/aromatherapy

Mittelmark, M. B., & Bauer, G. F. (2016). The Meanings of Salutogenesis. *The Handbook of Salutogenesis*, 7–13. https://doi.org/10.1007/978-3-319-04600-6_2

Moore, C. (2019). "Positive Daily Affirmations: Is There Science behind It?" *Positive Psychology.* positivepsychology.com/daily-affirmations/.

Patridge, C. (2014). The Occult World, 1st edition (ebook). Routledge Publ. ISBN 9781315745916. Doi: https://doi.org/10.4324/9781315745916

PDQ Integrative, Alternative, and Complementary Therapies Editorial Board. (2005, October 24). *Aromatherapy With Essential Oils (PDQ®).* Nih.gov; National Cancer Institute (US). https://www.ncbi.nlm.nih.gov/books/NBK65874/

Perry, G. (n.d.). *The Two-Zodiac Problem: History, Analysis, and Solution.* Retrieved September 23, 2024, from https://talk.vonabisw.de/Perry/Zodiac.pdf

Reed, T. (2024, September 23). *Every Zodiac Element: Fire, Earth, Air & Water*

Explained. Almanac.com. https://www.almanac.com/zodiac-elements-fire-earth-air-water-explained

Simmons, R. & Ahsian, N. (2007). *The Book of Stones*. North Atlantic Books.

Sutter, P. (2024, January 31). *Zodiac: Signs, symbols, history, constellations*. Astronomy Magazine. https://www.astronomy.com/science/a-scientific-guide-to-the-zodiac-symbols-signs-and-flaws/

Tarot. (n.d.). *Your Zodiac Sign's Power Color*. Tarot.com. https://www.tarot.com/astrology/zodiac-sign-colors

UK National Association of Jewelers (n.d.). *Zodiac Birthstones Jewelry: Star Signs, Gemstones and Their Meaning*. Www.naj.co.uk. https://www.naj.co.uk/zodiac-birthstones-jewellery

US Department of Veteran Affairs. (n.d.). *Instructions for Focused Breathing*. https://www.ptsd.va.gov/apps/STAIR/Session1/docs/Session1Hand out_INSTRUCTIONS_FOR_FOCUSED_BREATHING_Session1HO-dg_edit.pdf

Verywell Mind. (n.d.). *Is Holotropic Breathwork Right for You?* https://www.verywell mind.com/holotropic-breathwork-4175431

WebMD Contributors (2021, June 28). *What Is Breathwork?* WebMD. https://www.webmd.com/balance/what-is-breathwork

Wikipedia Contributors. (2019, November 25). *Sun sign astrology*. Wikipedia; Wikimedia Foundation. https://en.wikipedia.org/wiki/Sun_sign_astrology

Woodward, L. (2023). *How to Meditate*. 53–74. https://doi.org/10.1002/9781394200665.part2

Zodiac Constellations | Constellation Guide. (n.d.). https://www.constellation-guide.com/constellation-map/zodiac-constellations/#:~:text=The%20northern%20zodiac%20constellations%20%E2%80%93%20Pisces

Zodiac definition (n.d.). Www.merriam-Webster.com. https://www.merriam-webster.com/dictionary/zodiac

About the Author

Oonah Mae Platt is an independent author and book publisher with a passion for empowering others through her words. With her rich professional portfolio as a licensed healthcare professional and complementary and alternative medicine (CAM) practitioner in the United States, Oonah blends her expertise in wellness with her love for spirituality and astrology. Her open-minded dedication to the study of astrology and her enthusiasm for New Age topics bring a fresh perspective and uniqueness to each of her books.

Oonah's publishing journey includes collaborations with reputable companies like JKK Books & Media, where she honed her craft and built an impressive portfolio. *Zodiac Self-Care Guide: ARIES* marks the debut of her exciting 12-book zodiac self-care series. Each book in the series is created to empower readers to align with their cosmic energy. When she's not writing, Oonah enjoys a vibrant life with her two biological and two adopted children. She finds inspiration in meditation, reading, and an eclectic mix of music genres which fuels her creativity for penning self-help guides and crafting fictional adventures.

Zodiac Self-Care Guide
Aries

(A Lifestyle Blueprint for Aries)

Oonah Mae Platt

9 798230 026792